WITHDRAWN

PARENTING for Education

Revised Edition

Youth Literature By Vivian Owens
　　HOW OSWA CAME TO OWN ALL MUSIC
　　I MET A GREAT LADY
　　I MET A GREAT MAN
　　NADANDA THE WORDMAKER
　　THE ROSEBUSH WITCH

Nonfiction Books by Vivian W. Owens
　　CHEMISTRY QUICKIES
　　CREATE A MATH ENVIRONMENT
　　PARENTING FOR EDUCATION
　　THE MOUNT DORANS

PARENT TEACHER
371.302
OWENS

PARENTING for Education

Revised Edition

Any Parent Can Teach Informally

Vivian W. Owens

Mount Dora, Flordia

McHenry Public Library District
809 N Front Street
McHenry, IL 60050

PARENTING FOR EDUCATION
Revised Edition
Any Parent Can Teach Informally

By Vivian W. Owens

Published by:

ESCHAR PUBLICATIONS, LLC
P.O. BOX 1194, Mount Dora, Florida 32756
escharpub@earthlink.net
http://www.escharpublications.com

All rights reserved. No part of this book may be reproduced or transmitted in any form or by any means, electronic, or mechanical, including photocopying, recording, or by any information storage and retrieval system without written permission from the author, except for the inclusion of brief quotations in a review.

Copyright © 2013 By Vivian W. Owens
First Printing 2013
Printed in the United States of America

Library of Congress Catalog Card Number:2013935844

ISBN: 978-1-929221-01-1

Disclaimer: This book is written for the sole intent of expressing ideas on ways to improve learning for children. The information provided is not the only way. Neither the author or the publisher makes any representations, warranties, or guarantees about the success or lack thereof in the use and implementation of the books' content.

You may order single copied prepaid direct from the publisher for $21.95 plus $3.00 for postage and handling. (Florida residents add 7.0% for state sales tax). For terms on volume quantities, please contact the publisher.

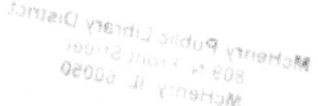

Dedication

To my children, April, Shea, and John (III), who have given me a special joy in "parenting for education."

Acknowledgements

I wish to thank Dr. Arlene A. Carter and Carolyn Maxwell, who remained faithful and dedicated in providing quick feedback, as I revised the original book, PARENTING FOR EDUCATION. Thanks, also, to Marilyn Orr, who shared photographs.

Cover Design by Nicole Greenwald

Interior Design by Nicole Greenwald

Introduction   1

Chapter 1   5
Let Home Say "Yes!" To A Good Learning Environment

- Kudos to Working Moms 7
- Parental Attitudes and the Child's Learning Environment 8
- 10 Ways To Provide A Nurturing Climate 10
- Your Child's Productive Use of the Internet—Sit in the Director's Chair 13
- Competent Learning 16
- Conversations 17
- Control of the Environment 18
- Okay! He's In School. What Now? 20
- Create A Math Environment For Your Child - Part I 22
- Toys Motivate Learning 24
- School's In: "Basic Level Of Learning" 25
- Take Time 27
- 25 Ways to Motivate Your Child for a New School Year 29
- Learning 32
- Expect Something Good 33

Chapter 2   39
Guidelines for Heading Learners in the Right Direction

- "Babies In Arms" Learning 41
- Increase Your Child's Common Knowledge 44
- Improve Reading Skills 48
- Manipulative Learning 49
- Provide a Vision for Your Children 51
- Reading Foundation 53
- Reasoning Situations 54
- Training Memory 56
- Vocubulary Enrichment 57
- Writing Preparation 58
- Activities Helpful In Laying A Reading Foundation 60
- Scope Of Reading 61

i

Counting 62
Give Meaning to Homework 63
Visualizing And Observing.. 64
Reinforcing Good Behavior 65

Chapter 3   71
Root Problems Of Learning & Their Solutions

Antidotes for Failure 73
Fix the Problem. Encourage the Child. 74
Focus Attention: Eliminate Distractions 76
Task Sequence 77
Organize The Disorganized Child 78
Time management 80
Be Quick 81
Overcoming Vagueness.. 82
How To Relieve Drudgery When Learning Hard Concepts........ 84

Chapter 4   89
Exercises to Raise Academic Performance

Tips To Help Parents Select Children's Literature...................... 91
26 Ways To Strengthen A Weak Memory In Classroom Learning.. 92
Holiday Sum Fun 96
Science in the summer 97
Reading That You Act Out.. 98
Educational Games 99
Classroom Success Strategies.. 101
Testing Success.. 103
Encourage Your Creative Thinker 104
Memory And Learning 106
Make Long Words Short... 106
Make Arithmetic Touchable 107
How To Make The Recall.. 108
Create a Mathematical Environment, Part II........................... 109

Chapter 5   115
How To Deal With Underachievement

    Clashing With The Underachiever 117
    "Gifted" Underachievers 119
    "Apathetic" Underachiever 122
    Where Does Marcia Fit In? 123
    When Kids Need to Figure Out What They Don't Know 125
    Nanette Slipped Through The Tracks 127
    Close the Educational Gap With Better Classroom Discipline . 129
    Close the Achievement Gap: Another Visit With Discipline" .. 130
    Close the Achievement Gap: Ambition Shifts 132
    "Unaware Optimist" Underachiever 134
    Prepare Children to Test Successfully 135
    Proven Strategies for Test-Taking 138

Chapter 6   143
Special Problems That Interfere With Learning

    Information Storage And Retrieval 145
    Are Medical Problems Interfering With Learning Or School
    Performance 146
    Help For Dyslexia 148
    Is Your Teen Depressed 149
    Cee-Cee's Puzzling Behavior 150

Chapter 7   155
Future Goal Setting

    Setting Achievement Goals 157
    A Dollar's Worth of your Time 158
    Is College In Your Future? 160
    Connect Intellect 161
    Financing A College Education 162

Chapter 8   169
Social, Cultural, And Civil Umbrella

    Socialization Of Our Young 171
    Experiences That Count 172
    Unreadiness In Children 173
    Reinforce Good Behavior 174

Chapter 9   179
Physically Arrange Your Home For Learning

    Use The Kitchen In Your Home 180
    Use The Living Room In Your Home 181
    Use The Bedroom In Your Home For Studying 182
    Use Your Office Space To Allow Your Child To Study 183
    Set Up A Basement Study Nook Or An Attic Study Nook 184
    Use Your Dining Room For Homework 185

Chapter 10   191
Plan Your Next Step

    Plan Ahead 193
    Unscramble The College Process 195
    College Is Your Choice 197
    Schools You Should Know 199
    AIM 202
    Choosing The Right College 203

Glossary of Terms   209

Index   222

Introduction

During my long career as a classroom teacher, I never met a parent who did not want his/her child to become a successful learner. Simultaneously, I have met many parents who did not know how to assist their children in the learning process. Wealthy, super-intelligent parents did not always know how to help their children—nor did career- successful parents. Poorly educated parents with few resources also struggled; and middle of the road parents shared similar problems. These realizations of whose children fared better in the educational arena taught me to look for common denominators in the parenting process. After all, if parental wealth, intelligence, and career success were not the direct source of student achievement in learning, then there must be other parameters, some visible and others less visible. I found myself studying families of children who performed well in the classroom. Perhaps, what these parents were doing naturally would shed light for other parents. Hard to ignore were the following: Certain values, certain attitudes, certain taught behaviors, specific interactions between parent and child, and defined expectations and goals. My informal study led me to formulate Parenting For Education (PFE).

Nearly thirty years have passed since Parenting For Education first aired as a local radio program, and it is now time that I revise my presentation, simplify approaches, and emphasize new concerns in education. At its core, PFE remains the same. Luckily, an accrual of thirty years has given me greater insight into what works for students and what hampers them.

Parenting For Education is an approach to education that emphasizes the parent's role in aiding the learning process for children. PFE seeks to motivate, inspire, and encourage parents to do all they can in the home environment. It encourages responsibility and commitment. Recognizing that parents contend with jobs and employment, giving them little time to do all they would want to do, PFE shows them how to maximize time they do have. Foundation learning in the home leads to confident academic performers. In the home, parents can make a huge contribution to their children's development of skills and performance goals needed for classroom success.

Whether you're the parent of a cuddly newborn or the parent of an independent adolescent, you can help your child make gains at whatever level he currently operates. That is to say, if you're the father of a twelve year-old who is not reading, you may apply ideas from "Reading Rites"

"Introduction"

in the same step-by-step manner as the father of a four year-old, who is just learning to read. The Parenting for Education philosophy emphasizes that we take children where we find them. It would be silly to force a low-reading skills sixteen year-old to explain a high level novel, when it would be more helpful to teach him vocabulary strategies others may have learned at age six.

This new edition of Parenting for Education offers a streamlined look at some of the ideas presented in the First Edition. It offers short essays aimed at showing how, why, and what problems your learner faces. Linked with the problems are the solutions. Because we, as parents, often become blind to our children as they participate in the classroom, some of my essays bring you into the classroom and allow you to witness your child and his classmates as a teacher might see them.

Like many of you, I share a deep concern that testing must be balanced with sincere and meaningful learning. Yet, testing is a factor requiring every parent's attention. Twelfth Grade is too late to look at your child's test scores and say, "I wish I had met with Chad's teachers after his 9th Grade test." Several essays will address some of the problems that may interfere with student test performance. Hopefully, you will harness an idea that you can use as your family moves through the testing process.

Finally, PFE comes to you as a creative thinking tool. Nothing that I say in this book is law. Nothing lies in stone. Ideas presented here should nudge you to think about your specific needs for your child, or perhaps ideas will open your eyes to a problem you had seen but had not acknowledged. In your hands, may this book gather energy of thought and love, which will prove beneficial to your children. I am happy to invite you to read Parenting for Education.

What is Parenting for Education?

Parenting for Education (PFE) is the philosophy that embraces a nurturing-teaching role for parents. It says that parents can carry out goals and activities in the home, which lead to better performance for the child in school. Parents who actively think about their children's learning needs make a big difference in their children's lives. Caring should enter into communication and guide all relationships. Issues of competence, home environment, time management, self-discipline, classroom cooperation, self-respect, self-responsibility, and motivation direct our goals with as much force as the actual strategies for learning subject content.

At any age a child benefits from a PFE Philosophy. The goals of parents of babies often coincide with the goals of parents of fourteen year-olds. Each parent seeks to know the strengths and weaknesses of his/her child, making it easier to praise and support effectively.

As the school year begins, consider setting aside time for each child on a daily basis. You are in the best position to give your child individual, unshared time. This is not an easy task for working parents, but you will find fifteen minutes spent with your thirteen year-old daughter makes both of you happier over the long haul. You may ask her to show you how to solve a math problem that appears in her class work notes or she may ask you to call out vocabulary words for English or Spanish class. Daily fifteen-minute conversations with your seven year-old son or your sixteen year-old son might inspire his confidence to participate in classroom discussions.

In addition to spending time together on a daily basis, consider checking to see that homework is completed on a regular schedule. Review graded papers with your child as soon as they are received. If possible, visit your child's school and contact his teacher, allowing for an early positive exchange. Communication proceeds rapidly when teachers see parents actively involved. With this demonstrated interest and support your child starts a school year of plusses.

While your child goes about his day, he practically hears your voice saying, "Act like a model citizen in the classroom and in school hallways. Pay attention in class, listen carefully, ask questions, and participate in all activities the teacher gives. Show respect for your teacher, yourself, and others. Cooperate fully and demonstrate a good attitude."

Ultimately, your efforts to parent for education will help create a stronger community and help instill important values in our children. Parenting for Education breeds competent, self-confident young people.

"Introduction"

Perhaps you are the parent of a baby or a preschooler, and your child does not participate in a formal school program. That's fine. Parenting for Education cherishes little ones and offers a wide lens across their growth and development. If you are home-schooling your children, the PFE Philosophy applies to your children with the same passion as children in formal school settings.

Hopefully, children of all ages and from a broad spectrum of backgrounds will gain a stronger place in whatever educational system they find themselves, because of the efforts made to incorporate ideas from the Parenting for Education Philosophy.

Chapter 1

Let Home Say "Yes!" To A Good Learning Environment

"Let Home Say, "Yes!" To A Good Learning Atmosphere"

PARENTING for Education

Kudos to Working Moms

Working moms, like Doris, come home tired at the end of a busy day, often having no desire to cope with their children's needs.

While Doris rode the elevator up to her apartment, she thought about the evening that lay ahead with her four children. Wearily, she wondered if she felt too tired to listen to ten year-old   play her flute—Josetta frequently played wrong notes. What about seven year-old Mikel? Would he want her to spin the globe and pin a country that he named? Sighing, she thought how proud she felt every time the boy revealed his knowledge of a foreign country. Actually, seventeen-year-old Jimmy Charles usually played "Spin the Globe" with Mikel, and later he would need her to critique his speech. Since Jimmy Charles debated on the school's team, he continuously prepared speeches. Momentarily, as the elevator door opened, Doris' thoughts turned to Anne Lea, her three year-old, who stayed with Great Aunt LouLea all day. She felt worried because Anne Lea could not talk very clearly and did more pointing than talking.

Undoubtedly, Doris' four children need her to nurture and guide them daily, but she finds the demands difficult and frustrating. Before she can engage in Parenting for Education, she needs help.

Help for Doris comes through anti-stress maneuvers for the entire family. Begin by setting priorities for daily living. List those values and principles you want to transmit to your children and think of how these values can be achieved. Examine the hindrances, which keep you and your family from these values-principles. For example: If one of your values is family good will, and lack of close-knit time hinders it, you

"Let Home Say, "Yes!" To A Good Learning Atmosphere"

need to write down your time schedule and see what activities can be eliminated in order to find more close-knit time.

Knowing your values and principles and knowing the hindrances that prevent your achieving them allow you to set a priority for activities you want to engage you. For Doris, priorities may include setting a quiet time of one half-hour for all family members, immediately after she arrives and greets everyone. This gives her time to refresh and rekindle good spirits. Dinnertime with all the family may be next on the evening's agenda, with the dinner meal having been prepared earlier using a crockpot. With all hands clearing away dinner dishes, everyone is soon free to complete other important tasks. Doris, then, finds time to spend with each child individually. Since she feels rested, she listens better and copes better. By the time her children are in bed, she is ready for her own personal activity.

In the long run, Doris' children benefit from any anti-stress maneuvers she conjures up for the entire family.

Parental Attitudes and the Child's Learning Environment

We all learn better if we feel comfortable and secure; children are no exception. A happy, well-adjusted child responds to a good environment with growth in a positive direction. As parents, we can do a lot to help our children move in this positive direction by providing a home which allows them to feel cared for and loved. Our parental attitudes often shape the learning environment. Our parental attitudes pour a foundation for learning.

Frequently, parents say, "Okay. I have the right attitude, but how do we show love when we're trying to incorporate

PARENTING for Education

learning in our home/ How do you mix love with A B C s?" Good question.

See if the following ideas seem doable in your home:

- Hold and snuggle the newborn through infancy as much as possible. Don't be afraid you're spoiling him. In fact, most children up to five years old need a great deal of holding and snuggling. Let it be a give-take love. Allow him to hug you when he feels like it. Of course, this is called "healthy touching." School aged children, whether third grade or high school junior, also need affection and show of concern.

- Laugh often. Laughing is infectious, and it spreads a joyful spirit throughout the child's being.

- Smile at him for no reason at all, except to show good will. It shows your good feelings about him—that he is a worthwhile, important individual just because he is himself. Smile also to show him you are particularly pleased with him for a special reason.

- Play with him every chance you get. The kind of play will naturally depend on the age group. If he's one year old or older, join in with his activity. Allow him to be the leader, dictating to you. Your third grader might enjoy a game of basketball and your high school junior would enjoy a board game or a computer game with you once in a while.

- Speaking to your child in tender, loving tones assures him that he is in friendly, kindly territory.

- Telling a child that you love him has to be the warmest and best assurance he receives from you.

Let us not be negligent in taking care of our children's physical needs. Food, shelter, and clothing should be their right.

9

"Let Home Say, "Yes!" To A Good Learning Atmosphere"

Children should not have to contend with adult problems. Don't burden them with problems that are out of their control.

Parental attitudes can have a positive effect on the child's learning environment. Healthy, positive parental attitudes stimulate healthy, positive attitudes in children.

10 Ways To Provide A Nurturing Climate

Walk into any home and you immediately feel good vibes or bad vibes. It's all about how you feel, because you will respond to an environment based on how you feel about it. Also, you respond based on how it made you feel. When you name the reasons you like coming into a particular setting, what reason heads your list? Did you name "comfortable" or "bright and cheerful"? Maybe you said that you felt it was all right for you to sit on the sofa and prop up your feet. For everyone, different reasons may prevail. As a parent, you will evaluate these reasons because they offer a guide to how you can turn your home into a nurturing climate for your children's educational welfare. Please review the ideas below and adjust the list to suit your lifestyle.

Physical Comfort is important. Design at least one area of your home that can hold children, books, and toys comfortably. Set up a space where children can plop on the floor and play games, where they can tumble and rollover, or hop on one leg. Organize shelves with favorite books that can be leisurely read. Is there a rough and ready sofa to leave in this space?

Mental comfort breaks the fall. Send out words and messages that welcome and invite your children to rest and play and have fun.

Emotional comfort can come through your gestures & attitudes. Attitudes of love, glad you're here, hope, warmth, care, and kindness generate unique sparks in people that uplift spirits and soothe emotional distress. In fact, the right attitude creates emotional comfort for all. Children are quite good at reading your hand gestures or body gestures or facial expressions that tell whether you're happy or sad or mad or displeased, so be careful with unspoken language as you work to give emotional comfort.

Show value of the nurturing spirit. For parents who grew up in homes devoid of encouragement or pats-on-the-back, it's sometimes hard to relax with your children and to find the right words to wash them in sunlight. Pulling a child to you, gently squeezing his shoulders, and saying, "Hmmm. You're wonderful. What a great hoop shot!" is difficult for some. You start by deciding that the nurturing spirit is a value that you want in your home. If it is a value, then you will find ways to show that value—just take that first step of wanting to sincerely give your child a sense of high self-esteem.

Plan activities that allow you to spend time together. In each other's presence, you have the opportunity to sow seeds of good will. You have the opportunity to train your child in ways that represent your family's values; and you have unlimited time to educate your child on numerous topics. At the end of a long walk or a fishing expedition, your son may gain confidence in himself and he may gain confidence in you.

Implement changes; improve the odds for your child's successful academic journey. No journey is completely smooth, as you usually find a few bumps in the road and snags from overgrown bushes. Maybe you've noticed temper tantrums flaring up when your child doesn't get his/her way or maybe you've developed a concern about poor reading habits. Maybe you've noticed some serious learning problems

"Let Home Say, "Yes!" To A Good Learning Atmosphere"

that only a professional can adequately address. Vow to implement changes. See what you can do to change problems into "former problems." Find the right help; find solutions. By building a nurturing environment, you embrace your children with all their faults, and you commit to changing the undesirable. As you implement change, you improve the odds for your child's successful academic journey.

Give respect. While you acknowledge that you want your child to enjoy high self-esteem, you seek ways to provide activities and materials that help him/her to leap forward at full speed. As you do this, consider how to convey a sense of respect to your child so that others will also respect her/him. Children also need to respect themselves and others as they grow up. In giving respect, we learn to show respect.

Choose "Growable" alternatives. Nurturing our children to become good citizens, leaders in the community, champions of their schools, good friends, good neighbors, good family members, and generally good people requires us to think ahead. We do not create citizens and leaders over night. Rather, we grow these virtues a little at a time, day-by-day, year-by-year. Our task is choose the "growable" alternatives; and this means asking ourselves what character traits can we promote and model that will lead to such end results.

Eliminate power bickering over minor problems. Throughout your parenting years, you're going to encounter many obstacles to maintaining good relationships with your children. One or more of your children may possess a strong, willful personality that will counter rules and challenge your actions. Often, during the teen years, if not before, parents and children come to blows. They find it difficult to reach agreement over simple issues and nearly battle over big issues. Keep in mind that you are the parent, but you need flexibility and broader outlook than your young charge. You want peace

PARENTING for Education

and harmony to prevail in a nurturing environment. Develop a sense of humor, engage in dialogue, and expand your patience in order to see your child's point of view. Through a gathering of your greater self, you will find ways to eliminate bickering over minor problems. Always leave the door open for discussion. Peace and happiness often require work.

Add features to daily living, which suggest fun. "All work and no play make Johnny a dull boy" is an old cliché worth examining. For children, as well as adults, routines can become boring and sometimes need spice to liven up things a bit. Ask your children which activities they would like to engage in occasionally. Ask them to show you something of interest to them. Ask them to tell you about their friends and about school. What music do they enjoy? Are they playing music regularly and inviting you to listen? Is there a special day of the week or month when the family goes out to dinner or to see a movie or attend a sports game? Examine your daily living and come up with ways to enrich your lives so that years from now, your children will say, "That was fun!"

Your Child's Productive Use of the Internet—Sit in the Director's Chair

Catherine, a young mother of four, expressed concern that the Internet may cause her children more harm than good. Bob, a forty-something father of teenagers, shares her worry. They are not alone. In a recent survey, more than 65% of parents said they dreaded bad things overpowering their children on the Internet. If you, too, are worried about Internet corruption, you may want to approach the problem with the lens of a director. Think in terms of personally directing your child's use of the Internet.

"Let Home Say, "Yes!" To A Good Learning Atmosphere"

Having raised three inquisitive youngsters, who enjoyed their alone time and did not appreciate parental intervention, I understand your apprehension. More than ever, parents have good reason to be wary of inappropriate content or contact children may encounter in cyberspace. The key is to productively channel your children's Internet activities in a manner that strokes their egos. You do this by introducing them to useful sites on which they will become hooked; and in this hooked state, they develop expertise. Potentially, directed sites can open their eyes to vast amounts of useful information they do not already know but have an interest in learning. Here are a few strategies to build your child's depth and breadth of knowledge about current events, history, economics, and global culture.

Hook your child on CNN.com or another global news web site. Poke your head in and ask your daughter if she can just check the news to let you know the latest breaking news on a topic about which she has an opinion—the presidential candidates, the Middle East situation, the economy/potential recession, or other current news head line. Ask what she thinks are the most important issues facing this nation.

Guide him to use the online encyclopedia, Wikepedia.org, to quickly bring you up to speed on people or historical events you should know about but don't. You might request that he brings you up to date on How the United Nations is organized and funded, the names and backgrounds of the current Supreme Court Justices, the intricacies of the Balkan or Gulf Wars, or how the caucus system works. Ask questions that solicit his opinion and encourage him to think about what he has just read and why that might be relevant to things he cares about.

Share your dream vacation with your children. Let them fill in the picture. Direct them to the Conde Nast Traveler or to National Geographic web site and have your daughter or son put together the perfect itinerary for that safari through Namibia or a trek through the Himalayas. Ask your son to describe his dream vacation, and ask him questions requiring further, more detailed research.

Highlight your savings goal with your children. Ask them to consult the personal finance links on the major search engines, so that they may advise you on which bank is going to give you the best rate on your preferred money market accounts. Ask them to determine which mutual funds have the lowest fees and highest returns? Point them to good articles on saving strategies and then pose this hypothetical question. "How should you invest $5,000.00, based on all you have learned from the financial web sites like Kiplinger.com?"

Show them how to use the Internet to find information on movies. Let your son consult moviefone.com to find two interesting independent films. Then, persuade him to tell you why those two films caught his attention.

Tell your daughter that you're trying to watch more PBS documentaries or historical dramas. Would she find two or three interesting programs on television for the coming week using pbs.com? With this ploy, you may gain a new television critic.

When we choose the director's chair instead of fears' lenses, we move into a more comfortable parental role. We provide a modicum of wide exploration on educational issues that may turn our children into the best possible Internet geeks.

"Let Home Say, "Yes!" To A Good Learning Atmosphere"

Competent Learning

The best learners in school or on the job or elsewhere are those who want to learn, those who believe they can learn, and those who are willing to learn.

From where do the desire and belief and willingness come?

You, the parent, can inspire your child to learn. Start by giving him confidence in himself. At the end of a day ask him what he's learned in a particular subject. Let's say, you ask him what project he's working on in Social studies. Encourage him to tell you about it, and while he's talking, show interest. Show interest and patience. Then, praise him. Let him know how wonderful it is for him to learn.

When you know your child is required to learn his multiplication tables, offer a reward along the path to the finished product. For instance, after he learns his two's, reward stickers. Three's, reward a movie or recreational treat. Four's, a small toy is appropriate. Five's, reward a favorite book.

Build your child's confidence by making him competent. Competence comes by studying and learning. Learning becomes a habit after some practice.

Confident, competent learners have the added benefit of good self- image. Isn't this what you want for your precious child?

Conversations

Most of baby's wakeful, playful hours are spotted with moments of babbling. Babbling is a language in its own right. It has rhythm and pitch according to the object baby is addressing. Quite often baby can be observed babbling softly to his own hand as he holds it in the air. At other times, he can be seen babbling quickly in high pitch to a toy, which keeps moving away from him. This babbling is paced by the patterns he has imitated from significant others.

Because he is already partaking in the communication network, imitating speech patterns and listening, he is eager to engage in a dynamic one-on-one conversation. Conversation with baby is only an extension of the talks mother began with the one-day old infant. The main difference is that now you expect him to answer.

Expect baby to answer and he will answer. Say something to him and wait a few minutes for him to answer. When he answers, you say something again, and then wait for him to answer again. Continue this procedure for five or more minutes.

Eye contact is essential. Laugh during the course of the conversation. Make expressions with your face and hands in your normal manner as when conversing with another adult. These kinds of exchanges give your baby a full appreciation of your awareness of him as an individual and of your awareness of his importance.

The more you engage baby in conversations, the more socialized he becomes. Experience shows that conversation contributes to broadening mental development and quickening mental alertness. The reasons are obvious: (1) any time anyone talks with you for several minutes, you use imagination

"Let Home Say, "Yes!" To A Good Learning Atmosphere"

to picture places or events described. (2) Conversation uses recall and memory of previous experiences linked to the present topic. (3) Language in its diversity of sounds and uses acclimatizes an individual to his environment.

Try to remember that conversation with peers involves a variety of sentences. Do not mainly state facts; ask questions, too. Show surprise sometimes. Vary the tone of your voice to fit the content. And make yourself sound interesting. Baby will definitely respond if you're interesting.

Control of the Environment

Giving a baby the feeling he is in control of his environment is not an easy thing to do, simply because most parents resist granting even a minute's worth of decision-making to young children.

Decision-making on simple matters like what to eat, what to play, or where to sit is the first part of a series of devices the eight to eighteen month old baby seeks in gaining control of his environment. His brain tells him he has power to choose, and he wants that power.

He needs that power in order to develop into a self-assured, self-directed individual. His power over his environment need not diminish your power. Rather, it should complement yours and should be viewed as a joint venture. In this respect, you maintain position as overseer, thus ensuring baby's safety.

Control of environment implies that the overseer grants two important rights to baby: Freedom to do and comfort to do.

"Freedom to do" means that mother allows baby to go where he wants, to choose his objects of interests, to choose his activities, and to carry out his activities on chosen objects in chosen locale. It means restraints are lifted, both physical and emotional.

Baby exercises the right to choose his favorite book during reading time, to choose orange juice instead of apple juice, his stroller, to play alone instead of in a group, to hold onto his toys rather than sharing them.

In a hundred different ways, baby assumes a leadership role wherein he chooses and dictates. With provisions furnished by mother, he will quickly learn an infinite amount about his own likes and dislikes as well as something about how his behavior influences another's behavior.

Many times aggressive behavior is going to dominate his personality, but this should be accepted as a positive sign in his growth pattern. That kind of behavior has a distinct and superior value in molding leadership characteristics. Leadership characteristics do not suggest bossy, domineering, repugnant people. They suggest people who are capable of handling their problems; people who meet their responsibilities; people who can manipulate any situation to the best advantage.

In order for a child to reach the point of being termed "aggressive" or "leader," he requires rearing in a nurturing environment, which fosters his controlling his environment.

Nurturing environments are crucial in order for baby to have "Comfort to do." "Comfort to do" describes the quality of attitudes, which prevail around baby during his moments of "doing."

Attitudes, which give him comfort, are saturated with understanding of his needs, kindness, and willingness to stand out of the way. He is alert to attitudes by way of voice tones, facial expressions, general mood, and by direct commands.

"Let Home Say, "Yes!" To A Good Learning Atmosphere"

But...you're saying, "How does this work? I can't permit a two-year old to decide what she's having for breakfast."

Actually, you introduce choice by saying, "Mary, we have scrambled eggs or wheat germ for breakfast. Which do you prefer?" In essence, you present the choices to your child, after you have already selected equally suitable choices. When she makes her selection, you have that privilege of nodding approval, as you want to show her she that made a very good choice.

If the idea of allowing the baby to control his environment causes you to tremble with a fear of "Sparing the rod and spoiling the child," consider the following.

- Most children who feel in control of their environments gain a sense of self worth and better adapt to learning socially acceptable behaviors.

- Most children who feel in control of their environments can be approached on a reasoning level more maturely than their counterparts.

What do you say to a baby's control of his environment? Are you willing to try it? Good Luck!

Okay! He's In School. What Now?

You've probably done a good job with your child up to this point. With the advent of school, many parents falsely believe, "It's now up to the teacher. She'll teach Johnny. I don't have anything to worry about." The fact is this: Johnny is still yours, and you should keep an eye on him. You are the overseer of his education. Your diligence might make the difference between his success and failure.

PARENTING for Education

Successful learners need strong moral support. Going off to school is not easy for a lot of little ones; they would rather curl up in front of the television or play outdoors with pets. When they find themselves in a strange new world of unfamiliar faces and rules and regulations and extra demands, they want to take wings and fly to distant shores. Insecurities, jealousies, missing nap time, missing Mommy and baby sister, and missing a special snack all add up to an unhappy beginning.

Offer your child moral support by tuning in to his feelings about school. Allow him to vent his frustrations or anger. Sympathize! Empathize! Listen. Ask what you can do to help.

At the backbone of your moral support is your own awareness of the school where you've enrolled your child. Have you studied the school's policy handbook? Do you know the principal? Did you go up to the teacher and introduce yourself? Do you know the curriculum plan for your child's grade? Do you know the schedule of activities for the school year? Have you taken the time to leaf through textbooks? What about snacks and lunches?

If your awareness passes muster, you probably have a good attitude about the educational system. Great! Every child needs a parent with a good attitude about the whole process of education, for a parent's good attitude rubs off on the child. We owe it to each child to instill positive values about educational institutions, his teachers, his classmates, his books and his lessons. Since most of his waking hours will be spent in school for the next twelve years, help him to enjoy the place.

Parent, your child needs you.

"Let Home Say, "Yes!" To A Good Learning Atmosphere"

Create A Math Environment For Your Child - Part I

"Math is hard! I just don't get it," Suzy says. Eric supports her statement by saying, "I don't expect to get good grades in math. Mom says she never understood it."

Don't we all look forward to the day when children will say, "Math is simple? It's like taking candy from a baby."

Poor progress and wilting frustration over math can be avoided if parents began exposing their children to math concepts at an earlier age. Exposure involves looking at numbers and the way they work in terms of things the child sees, feels, touches, and hears. The child makes this sensory response best under comforting, normal circumstances without pressure. He learns math as part of his usual, daily routine. He is made aware of number relationships within the simple network of family living.

Here's how:

When the table is being set for a meal, allow your child to help. Rather than saying, "Take out plates and forks," you say, "Take out four (4) plates and four (4) forks." Show him to associate a number with a set of objects. Count aloud, pointing and touching as you go along.

When family members intend being absent from the dinner table, allow your child to tell you for how many people you need to prepare.

Make estimates of distance in terms of feet and yards if you're around home. While in a car, on the bus, or walking, speak of distance from one place to another in terms of miles or fractional miles.

PARENTING for Education

Invite your child to help you make cookies. She can learn to add, multiply, and divide without ever using these terms. Select recipes that call for easily handled numbers. For example: One recipe bakes 45 cookies. Take out 3 long cookie sheets. Allow the child to decide how many cookies each sheet will hold, how many cookies to place in a row, and how many rows.

Measuring utensils offer an introduction to or practice with conversion units.

On the day before marketing, persuade your fifth grader to look over the sale sheet of the newspaper. Discuss how much it costs to buy 3 gallons of milk if the price of one gallon is $4. Decide whether to buy Brand X or Brand Y which has comparable quality, if Brand X costs 3 cans for 90 cents and Brand Y costs 4 cans for $1.

Ask Zoey to hang clothes vertically or to lie something horizontally. In play, suggest that she line up two pencils or two chairs at and angle. Help her cut out square pieces of nubby fabric. Toss her a cube of ice.

In sharing candy or in cutting pies, you show ½ candy bar or pie. Illustrate fractional parts by reading one-third of a book to your child or picking up one-tenth of his toys.

Mathematical language used in hands-on-activities helps the child to make recall or association later during abstract problem solving.

As commonplace as the above examples are, they demonstrate addition, subtraction, fractions, and division. Always keep numbers simple and solutions simple and logical. Do not get too involved. Let it go for another time if she does not comprehend what you're saying.

23

"Let Home Say, "Yes!" To A Good Learning Atmosphere"

Special time doesn't have to be set aside for teaching concepts using this approach, because you incorporate math activities into your daily routine by awareness that you can incorporate it easily. Begin math language and activities with your toddler. If your child is older, start there.

Toys Motivate Learning

Sit quietly for fifteen minutes in the presence of a child handling a toy. Do nothing but observe the child. Notice the development of motor skills for the one-year-old as she attempts to move the wheel on the toy car. Can you hear four-year old Brian talking to himself, as he corrects the problems in his leaning tower of Pisa that he's building with logs? Watch how three year old Terry decides which puzzle piece to use, as he tinkers with the "shapes" box. Keep your eye on the seven and eight year olds who have been erecting a bridge over the last several days.

If you take note of any child playing with toys, you have to conclude that toys motivate learning. In fact, toys are good investments for promoting thinking and reasoning skills.

Throughout my years of teaching, I noticed that my best physics or math students usually played with Lego or other structural building toys since their very early childhood. They usually enjoyed musical toys—like the piano, guitar, or horn. Radio kits, telescope kits, model airplanes, and put-together train sets figured prominently. Puzzles appropriate to a child's age always stir thinking and arouse curiosity. Games of all types, particularly those sold in educational toy stores, have the power to increase different learning skills.

Parents of babies aged one week to two years old should look for soft, cuddly toys in order to develop learning skills through touch, sight, and sound. Mobiles for this age group excite the imagination and prod language development. With any toy, parents are reminded to keep safety in mind. Avoid toys with features (pull-off buttons, for example) which would harm a young child.

Before you conclude your toy shopping, do buy a tape recorder for family use. Tape recorders come in handy for children wanting to listen to stories on audiocassette.

Whether you purchase toys on birthdays, Christmas, special holidays, or another time of year, please keep in mind that child's play is natural, good, and desirable. Every child needs toys because toys motivate learning and encourage healthy intellectual development.

School's In: "Basic Level Of Learning"

Green hulled walnuts will drop to the ground in my yard within a couple of weeks, and gray squirrels will scamper furtively, gathering the fallen walnuts. Rushing about in eager anticipation of storing their nuts, the squirrels remind me that fall is nearly here. Some mornings their chattering mingles with the chattering voices of little children travelling past my door on their way to school.

Little children on their way to school carry such promise in their bosoms. They're remembering good friendships, kind teachers, rocking chairs in the kindergarten classroom, and fun learning activities. They can't wait to get started. In their hearts, they step into a magic circle of "SCHOOL'S IN." You've been there. You know the feeling. I wish it were possible to keep the magic of the first day all year long. Parents might begin now to think of ways to help their children hang on to the promise of "SCHOOL'S IN."

"Let Home Say, "Yes!" To A Good Learning Atmosphere"

Think not of grades and test scores as the school year begins. Instead, think of individuals. Your child is a unique human being with feelings and needs unlike another. He needs your love, guidance, and support in order to rise to his best potential. You are the over-seer of his education, and good things happen when you take that responsibility seriously.

Celebrate your child's unique personality. Compliment him for the strengths that enable him to be a productive human being, and you increase his sense of self worth. You might say, "Gee! John, you're so good at organizing a room. You're a big help to me and to others." Go further by allowing John to use his organizational skills during family activities. He will carry over these strengths to the classroom in a variety of ways.

Build your child's ego. Show Leon how to meet responsibilities, how to arrive punctually for appointments, how to keep his word, how to attend his grooming and good health. In doing these, he will develop a good feeling about the way he interacts with others and will enjoy the respect and confidence people give him as a result of these actions.

Build your child's level of competence. Competent people succeed. Competency develops by practice. You can see to it that your first grader spells and reads because you can call out words to her and listen to her read. If she practices spelling and reading every day, she is bound to develop some competence. When you decide to oversee this competency development, you will make early contact with her teachers and school administrators. You want to stay informed about your daughter's needs and seek to improve deficiencies. Competent learners feel good about themselves, and they feel good about others. They must also know how to read. When was the last time you heard your fifth grader, seventh grader, or eleventh grader read? An older child who is not reading needs your help in eliminating that problem. Help him to become competent.

Set high standards. Show faith in your child's ability to do a good job in the school system. Children need to hear parents say, "I know you can do it!" Achieving goals is not always easy, but children do not give up when the road turns rocky if they know you believe in them. When you let your children know the good you expect, they work hard to reach higher. High standards reflect not only in grades, but also in good behavior, self- discipline, and in moral codes of ethics.

When parents think of ways to help their children hang on to the magic and promise of "SCHOOL'S IN," they find that they also reach new levels of satisfaction. Whether you're the parent of a six year old, twelve year old, or fifteen year old, your parenting role is important. Your diligence this year might prevent an unhappy, poorly adjusted first grader, or it might prevent your teenaged daughter from becoming pregnant. It might also turn on academic headlights for your middle schooler or prevent your high school son from turning to gang violence. Parents have more influence over their children than peer groups, television and other media, teachers, and all aggravators. Parents have the power to make good things happen for their children.

Take Time

Take time with your children, parents. They grow up all too fast. Diapers don't last forever, and teething pains come to an end. Your unruly two year-old quickly turns into a well-behaved first grader. So, enjoy each stage of their growth. Your memory of these days will be precious later.

"Let Home Say, "Yes!" To A Good Learning Atmosphere"

That spic and span floor you polish every day to impress your neighbor, that overtime pay you insist on making, those frequent club meetings you must attend, and the social functions you can't miss amount to only a grain of sand when compared with the rewards of parenting.

Twenty minutes a day to sit with your child going over the day's events, allowing him to tell you what was important, hearing his joys and frustrations, can be priceless. Playing bingo with the family, worshiping together, shopping with your teenaged daughter, watching your son play basketball, and baking a chocolate cake with your small fry are activities to cherish.

We take this time by first affirming that it is important to take time every day to be with your child in loving companionable communication. We schedule that time into our busy day's activities. It is said that the reason many parents have lukewarm affections for their children is due to failure to bond during infancy. They fail to spend enough time holding, feeding, nurturing, and loving the infant. I believe that a similar bonding must continue with our offspring until they reach adulthood. Bonding, to me, means

taking time to say, "I love you," to hug, to smile, to pat a hand, to dry a tear, to say a kind word, and to live in harmonious company with our children whatever their ages.

PARENTING for Education

25 Ways to Motivate Your Child for a New School Year

At the beginning of every school year parents want to look ahead to see how best to boost their children's morale for a fun academic journey. You want them to keep or build good self-esteem as they strive to study and learn amidst all of their other daily living involvements. What you ask yourself is this: How do I motivate my child for a new school year?

Consider using one or more of the following 25 ways to motivate your child for a new school year.

1. Encourage consistent, hard work.

2. Set an atmosphere, which allows comfort to fail, with the understanding that you pull yourself up and try again.

3. Encourage practice. Good scholars practice working math problems, analyzing political cartoons, or deriving word meanings.

4. Compliment attempts to think through situations.

5. Gently nudge children to understand the roots of their own behaviors and actions. Each student is responsible for his/her own behaviors and must accept consequences of those behaviors.

6. Share current news that excites you. Engage children in your excitement through discussion.

7. Offer choices whenever situations permit.

8. Invite your child's questions about anything. Assure him that any question that prickles his mind is worth exploring.

"Let Home Say, "Yes!" To A Good Learning Atmosphere"

9. Reward your child's completion of household chores in nontraditional forms. Integrate quality of performance with time delivery. For example: Assign your son the task of vacuuming, to be completed daily over a one-month period. Require him to daily evaluate the job he does. Show him what to look for and how to rank these performance measures. At the end of the month, if his vacuuming meets criteria you and he have set up, award privileges in the form of activities that will enrich him in some way.

10. Look for leadership opportunities within the home, school, church, and the at-large community. See to it that your child stays involved and interested in issues and activities that serve humanity. Her involvement will motivate her to take leadership roles as she sees needs.

11. Introduce your child one-on-one to people who love their jobs or their hobbies. Ask the chosen person to share an hour with your child, talking and showing her what he/she does.

12. Arrange for your child to accept a challenge that you know he can master. This need not be academic. Running one mile instead of a half mile is a challenge for some inactive middle-students. Reading poetry before the class is a challenge for some high school students.

13. Strengthen your child's weak academic area by providing continuous, regular, one-on-one tutoring by a qualified professional teacher who specializes in that academic area.

14. Provide the essential tools and materials for your child's academic program.

15. Make your home environment stimulating. Mira's home is filled with books, and she sees her father

reading constantly. Akeem's father and mother repair and rebuild car engines for fun. Creah's mother holds book club meetings in their apartment once per month. Neighborhood children often stop by to help Mrs. Jones with the pets she keeps. Her own children love to groom and train show dogs. Dinner conversations about world events or local politics dominate the Moore's home. Usually, the Moore children make a habit of reading the newspaper before dinner in order to contribute intelligently to conversation. Stimulating environments motivate children to learn and grow and reach for higher goals.

16. Monitor your teenager's job hours. The teenager who works 30 to 40 hours per week has trouble staying awake in class, and he has no time to prepare or study for classes. Make decisions about working goals before your child reaches an entrapment stage.

17. Start during the early years to teach your child a sport. Little league teams do a great job and are usually free to all, but children can play ball with you and the family or with other neighborhood children. To engage in a sport or to love a sport does not require that a child possess a great talent. Fortunately, even very ungifted players gain many benefits from sports' involvement.

18. Buy games and puzzles for the home. Help children learn how to play the game or to complete the puzzle. See to it that your children often use these games or puzzles.

19. Set reasonable expectations for your children. Share your expectations clearly with them, so that you're on the same wavelength.

20. Find out whether your child tests well. Perhaps he needs guidance in learning to prepare for and take tests.

"Let Home Say, "Yes!" To A Good Learning Atmosphere"

21. Show your child how to set and plan for goals.

22. Assist your child in developing a sense of time management.

23. Encourage your child to seek friendships with other children who share similar moral values and who have high aspirations.

24. Use words of encouragement to lift your child's morale. Use words of compliment to build higher self-esteem. However, do not lie to your child and foster a wrong or misguided self-perception.

25. Involve yourself in helping your child to study. This might take the form of the child teaching you a concept she has learned in a science class. Your frequent involvement allows you to pinpoint difficulties before they become serious.

Learning

Learning is the most important function of childhood and of youth, and it is the only means of achieving an education. We learn through formal and informal settings.

Formal settings are usually classrooms.

Informal settings can be anywhere, anytime, with anyone, at home, at church, in front of the television set, with Mom and Dad, with friends. Informal settings are usually unplanned experiences.

Informal learning can be as meaningful and as much fun as formal. That type of learning began the moment your child was born, and it continues through life. Therefore, take charge of your child's learning experiences—plan them, guide them.

Here are a few tips:

> If you have a baby, begin talking clearly to him right now. Sing to him. Read to him. Move him about. Let him see. Let him touch.
>
> If you have a toddler or preschooler, read to him. Talk to him. Take him to the zoo or the circus or to any interesting place. Expose him to different forms of culture. Give him a hobby.
>
> If you have children five to ten years of age, read to them. Let them read to you. Play games. Take them to interesting places. Tell them about their family tree. Teach them your morals and values. Teach them your hobby.

Let us think about some of the things that we want our children to learn in informal settings. Think what they might learn just idly watching men build at a construction site or watching a jeweler repair a watch. Under these relaxed conditions, you are able to engage their reasoning powers and imagination skills leading them toward memory, perception, intelligence, and other behaviors necessary in learning how to learn.

Expect Something Good

Call Betty "Smart" and she will think of herself as smart; preach Alex a sermon on his "dummy" brain, and he will know he's a dummy. Generally, children live up to your expectation of them. In many ways that's a frightening realization, for much harm can be done (and is). But in another sense, it offers powerful leverage to the parent who wishes to shape a terrific youngster.

33

"Let Home Say, "Yes!" To A Good Learning Atmosphere"

Shaping a terrific youngster comes through knowing your child's strengths and weaknesses, for you are then in a position to gauge your expectations in proportion to realism. For example, if Alex is a horrible speller, you should not scream at him for not being selected to the City Spelling Bee. On the other hand, you can begin calling words out to him three days prior to a class' spelling test, expecting him to make an "A."

If Pamela has always been top notch in figuring out word problems and quick with numerical calculations, you have a right to expect excellent grades in her mathematics report. Falling below the mark is unacceptable, and you let her know that. To reach and maintain her best performance, Pamela may need constant reminders that your expectations are based on your awareness of her true potential.

"Be true to you" is an old adage few children adhere to. It is much easier to be true to the peer group; and in so doing, they tend to expect less of themselves in relation to their true abilities. They need their parents to say, "I expect something good from you. So much about you is terrific."

Certain qualities have to be instilled in children before they or you can realistically expect something good. Following are examples of qualities that enable children to pursue maximum achievement:

- Habit of putting forth best effort
- Persistence
- Self confidence
- Winning attitude
- Goal setting habit
- Optimism

PARENTING for Education

"Let Home Say, "Yes!" To A Good Learning Atmosphere"

Make a Note:

What ideas from this chapter can you use?

_____

_____

_____

_____

List the tools and supplies that will help you start.

_____

_____

_____

_____

Is there a time in the day that's good for you and your child to work on this together?

_____

_____

When will you start?

Date to begin_____

Come Back Later

After you begin using ideas from this chapter, come here to this space to make notes on the outcome.

How did things go? Good ❑   Bad ❑   Indifferent ❑

What changes did you make? _____
_____
_____

How did your child respond? _____
_____
_____

What problems did you encounter and how did you handle the problem?
_____
_____

Overall, were you satisfied with the results you achieved?
_____

Did you meet your expectations? _____
_____

Chapter 2

Guidelines for Heading Learners in the Right Direction

"Guidelines for Heading Learners in the Right Direction"

"Babies In Arms" Learning

When do babies start learning? How do they learn? What do you teach them? All of these questions stir the minds of young parents.

You may assume that your baby is ready to learn at the moment of birth, when he is placed in your arms. Notice the way he looks at you, as you talk to him during those very early moments of life. Also, notice the instinctive way the baby sucks at his fist or holds tightly to your finger. Those observations suggest that the baby's brain activity is running and ready to go. It also tells you that nature has supplied him with some good instincts.

"Babes in arms" learning can be fun and enjoyable for you and your baby. The earlier you start a communication process, the more responsive your baby grows. With the bond developing between you, you discover a way to impart wholesome personal image, self- confidence, worthy values, and high self esteem.

A baby's learning is a natural, gradual process requiring no blackboards or computers, no fusses, and no hassles. What is required of you is a loving, kind feeling toward your baby and a warm, friendly attitude. You must decide that your baby is worth lots of your time and attention. You want to relax and properly care for your little one. Provide good health care and keep him safe in all environments in which you take him. Good nutrition, good sleep, good guardianship, and proper clothing are backdrops for the good learning that can take place.

Keep your baby near you, whenever possible, in order to strengthen emotional ties. Watch him grow under your nurturing care.

"Guidelines for Heading Learners in the Right Direction"

Examine the following strategies for stimulating babies to learn. Practice these routinely. See which ones work best for your family.

1. Start talking to your baby the moment he is born. Talk softly and soothingly. Tell him his name and his parents' names. Tell him where he lives. If there are other sisters or brothers, tell him about them.

2. Hold your baby closely as you talk to him.

3. Walk around the room, holding your baby and talking soothingly.

4. Sing all of the nursery rhymes that you remember. Sing any other songs. Usually, babies love all types of music.

5. Read aloud to your baby every day immediately after feeding time. You may read the evening newspaper, poems, bible verses, children's books, or anything you choose.

6. Sometimes during the day, turn on the tape player and play Handel's Water Music or Dance of the Sugar Plum Fairy. Actually, any music that is piquant and engaging.

7. Choose books from you local library that are colorful and pleasing to look at, even if you are sleepy. Read these daily to your baby of any age.

8. Buy some of the cloth books for your baby and allow her to hold and handle these whenever she pleases.

9. Play peek-a-boo games with baby.

10. Play patty-cake games with baby.

11. Place babies hands over your eyes, nose, and mouth, and call these by name. Example: "Feel my eyes."

PARENTING for Education

12. Sit with a six month old baby or older on a cushioned floor (rug or carpet) and roll a ball back and forth.

13. Allow the baby of any age to play with soft toys that do not have any sharp edges or detachable objects. Play is essential for any intellectual development.

14. Socialize the baby by permitting him to enjoy the company of other babies, other children, and adults.

15. Several times during the week, give your baby or small child learning sessions of "Touch the object." Use swatches of corduroy or velvet fabric and let him run his fingers across it. Dip her fingers into varying degrees of water, warm or cool or cold. Always talk to her to let her know what she is feeling.

16. Show your baby how to perform certain actions. "Clap!" "Rub your arm!" "Blow the soap bubble!"

17. Carry your baby into varied settings. Stroll through a museum. Browse through a bookstore. Swing at the park. Run through sand at a beach.

18. Consider the values to be derived from church attendance or from other places of worship. Your family may receive support and encouragement as you articulate the moral foundation you want to use in raising your child.

19. "Babes in Arms" learning quickly turns into toddler or preschool learning. It is the beginning step and needs your full attention. Time given to your baby matters. Be generous in spending time with him/her. Make that time positive and happy. Help your child to enjoy laughter. Let your child hear the sounds of laughter.

20. Enlist the help of your mate, family, and friends as you expose your child to learning. Ask them to read and talk

"Guidelines for Heading Learners in the Right Direction"

to the child, if the child is in their care. Ask them to point out objects and name them, even allowing the child to touch objects as naming occurs.

Many parents of happy, healthy, well-adjusted children will tell you that parents should be the main care givers for their children, particularly when children are under the age of three years old. Parents can offer loving concern and tender words which come from the heart. You make childcare something greater than mere custodial care. For working parents, this means carefully choosing childcare providers during your work hours and planning after-hours time with your child in a manner, which constantly enriches your child.

Most teachers will tell you that your child needs you. You can motivate your child and show strong interest in him/her. You help your children to succeed.

"Babes in Arms" learning starts your child and you on the right path to" Parenting For Education."

Increase Your Child's Common Knowledge

For kindergarten children, the storage tank of common knowledge may be quite different from that of fourth graders. The fourth grader's store of common knowledge may be different from that of an eighth grader, whose common knowledge is different from a twelfth grader's. So, age and grade level play a major role in determining what should a child already know when he enters a classroom. In your parenting role, you can checklist items for each of your children, determining whether each one possesses baseline knowledge. That baseline common knowledge will keep them from scratching their heads as often or from wondering what's going on and why they can't understand what everyone else is grasping easily.

Ways to communicate common knowledge comes through ordinary, every day living. Talking to your child gives him language and wider knowledge of the world around him. Take your child to the grocery store, bookstore, furniture store, electronic store, computer store, the post office, and other common places. Visit a church, a city park, or a zoo.

Introduce him to various careers or occupations, like a chef, a policeman, or a golfer. In a doctor's office, point out the secretaries, bookkeepers, nurses, technicians, and the doctor. At the pharmacy, discuss details of the pharmacist's job. Show your child how to recognize the dress of certain professions

Samples Of Common Knowledge For Different Age Groups

Kindergartener

1. Nursery rhymes, alphabet sing-song, color recognition, ring games
2. Names of family members, home address and contact information
3. Recognizes common animals: birds, dogs, cats, cows, horses, squirrels, and rabbits
4. Can distinguish between a school and a church
5. Can interpret traffic signals
6. Can ask simple questions to gain information.

"Guidelines for Heading Learners in the Right Direction"

Fourth Grader

1. Home address and contact information, Principal of his school, Governor of his state, President of the United States

2. Names of states, names of big cities in United States

3. Names of world places currently in the news

4. How to read newspapers

5. How to read simple books

6. How to add, multiply, and divide

7. How to tie his shoelaces

8. Knows how to carry out tasks for a simple project.

9. He should know more than younger children.

8th Grader

1. How to give directions to his home

2. How to read, how to write, how to do simple math

3. Shows reasonable skills in abstract thinking

4. Engages in critical thinking

5. Knows how to listen attentively for 20 minutes

6. Can discuss civic issues

7. Shows an awareness of science, particularly biology and earth science

8. Knows how to maneuver around the city or town where he lives.

12th Grader

1. How to read a book
2. How to figure out simple math problems for daily consumer living
3. How to solve basic algebra and geometry problems
4. How to read a newspaper
5. How to read a road map
6. Know basic information about government operations
7. Knows local laws
8. Possesses some literary knowledge
9. Shows an awareness of art & music
10. Possesses basic knowledge of sports and entertainment
11. Do all the things a younger child knows how to do.

When we find our children deficient in common knowledge, we do what we can to upgrade knowledge and skills by providing greater exposure and by enlisting help from our schools. Ask for help from your extended family in providing common knowledge to your children. Outside involvement in civic organizations, sports activities, children's theatre, Scouts, church, and other community groups will definitely expand your child's understanding of the larger world in which he lives.

"Guidelines for Heading Learners in the Right Direction"

Improve Reading Skills

Your own children may be adults by now, and you may be a grandparent. You may also be an aunt, uncle, or godparent. Maybe you're none of these, but you work with young children in a church or civic organization. I believe you play a tremendous role in carrying out messages of PARENTING FOR EDUCATION and you may also play a role in implementing the PFE Philosophy, because you can assist in nurturing educational values within any child whose life you touch. Consider how you can help a child learn to read or to develop and improve reading skills.

"Practice makes perfect" may be trite, but it's true. The more you do of anything, the better you do it. Reading is no exception. Good readers read frequently. Much depends on the child's age group.

The following suggestions are aimed at children who are already reading, however slightly:

1. If possible, make use of educational technology in the form of audio-visual material and equipment. Look for these in bookstores, electronic shops, toy stores, general stores, or computer stores.

2. Investigate computer software specifically geared to developing reading skills.

3. Play vocabulary games.

4. Visit the library. Children should use story cassettes and borrow story records for listening pleasure. Many records have follow-along books.

5. Use tape-recorders. Encourage your protégé to read a poem, nursery rhymes, or stories for taping sessions. Later, he can listen to them at his own leisure.

6. Train the child to create mental pictures as he reads or as he listens to others reading.

7. Role-play while reading.

8. Play sound games using certain vowel sounds or consonant blends.

9. Name as many words as you can that sound like sat—emphasize a.

10. Exercise your tongue with "CL": See if you can cluck like a chicken as you engage the child with you in this funny learning activity. Then, add different endings to "CL."

11. Read nightly bedtime stories. Even older children (7-12 years old) sometimes enjoy an adult reading to them, perhaps a popular book that's been made into a movie.

12. Make spelling a fun-for-a-minute affair. While you're turning off the lights in Danny's bedroom, ask him to spell "light;" while he's going off on his bicycle, call out a couple of simple words. Fun-for-a-minute spelling means one or two words at off-guard moments.

Manipulative Learning

A tall-tale teller might try to convince you he picked up an elephant and sat him in a hand-woven basket, or he might try to convince you that a rhinoceros weighs the same as a canary. But you would know he was lying, for you have a sense of comparative weights. You know what's heavy, and what's extremely heavy, and what's lightweight or medium weight.

"Guidelines for Heading Learners in the Right Direction"

How did you develop this sense of comparative weights?

Undoubtedly, you learned through the experiences of picking up or trying to pick up certain objects. So, let it be for your young ones. Allow them to manipulate objects around your home: picking up and holding, touching, pushing. Manipulation draws the child into making use of his intelligence. Lack of manipulation during preschool years slows your child's later learning abilities.

By touch alone, a toddler can learn to distinguish rough textures from smooth or grainy or slimy ones; he's able to identify warms, cool, soft, or dry. Active handling of objects is a precondition for a child's conceptual understanding and use of numbers.

Much of the manipulative experiences take place through play, and children learn best through play. Perhaps, as we play with a preschooler, we can incorporate the following activities:

1. Tying knots

2. Holding tiny objects and arranging them in different positions

3. Placing pegs in a pegboard.

The next time your little one pushes a chair across a floor, clap for him. The more he manipulates the better his understanding of the world around him.

PARENTING for Education

Provide a Vision for Your Children

As I grew up in a large family, my father continually repeated, "I want all of my children to have a trade. Beyond high school, each one has to become an expert in doing something. Every community needs a hairdresser, an auto mechanic, an electrician, a plumber, and other trained experts." When I was about ten years old and showed an interest in experimental cooking, my dad said, "You'll probably be a renowned chemist one day and create all kinds of new things the world has never heard of." Listening to his mantra of having my own trade, week after week, year after year, I soon realized that his vision needed to become my goal.

Pick up your newborn child and imagine a future for him. Imagine a future that holds wonderful things for your child and plant those ideas in your child's mind. Give details to the ideas. Start with early childhood basics, like the following:

Good behavior,

Stick-to-it skills

Quiet contemplation,

Think it through skills,

Good listening skills

In providing vision, you also provide a ladder showing the child how to reach his goals.

"Bobby, your behavior is going to be so good when you go to school. Everybody will say to me, "Mrs. McGill, your Bobby has the best home training of any of our students."

"Here, Nicole, complete this puzzle. You always want to complete a job and in that way, people can know this is who

"Guidelines for Heading Learners in the Right Direction"

you are. You will be reliable and dependable. You will always get the job done."

When you think of providing a vision for your children, not only do you think of the far-off future, but also think of nearby daily goals that must be met if future goals are to be obtained. You show a mental picture to the child of the best that he can be. You point out his strengths and you show appreciation for his strengths. You work to cultivate skills that enable him to become competent. You nudge your daughters and sons to master understanding concepts presented in the classroom.

Visions are structural outlines that encourage people and guide progress. Do not be afraid that your vision will place stress on your child or pressure him to succeed. Like me with my father's vision, your child will figure out his own route; your child will develop his or her own vision, after you have planted the seed. With vision, the child looks at every nook and cranny in the world to see what interests him the most.

From that point, he proceeds to acquire skills that consistently develop him into a competent practitioner of some art. In the classroom, he knows that he must develop better than adequate reading and math skills. If he aims for a scholarship, he will make sure that he studies and prepares for tests in order to perform at high levels.

On a dark, lonely road, most of us would welcome a beckoning, friendly light. A light that sweeps a wide arc draws us in and makes our path clear. A good vision is like a light in the dark. Parents have the opportunity to tell their children that good things await them. Parents have at least eighteen years with their children to continually show vistas of good living and of success that could belong to the child.

PARENTING for Education

Reading Foundation

Although some children are natural readers, most require help. Methods of teaching reading are as varied as the children learning to read, but generally they all employ sight or sound techniques – maybe both. In learning to read, a child uses purely mental tasks involving an interpretation of ideas from graphic symbols.

As in any building, certain foundation is essential:

- Child must have a sense of direction, as in moving from left to right.

- Child must have eye-hand coordination.

- Child must be able to recognize letters of the alphabet.

- Child must recognize a word as made up of letters.

- Child must recognize a sentence as made up of words.

- Child should be able to hear initial sounds of words.

- Child should be able to hear ending sounds of words.

- Child must be able to differentiate sounds of alphabet in their most familiar forms.

- Childs should be able to hear the short vowel sounds in short, simple words.

Some incidentals to a successful reading foundation might include: Imitative reading. A child who sees Mommy or Daddy, or other family reading will want to read. Continuous reading. Mommy of Daddy reading to Johnny on a daily basis will encourage him to read for himself later. Access to books. If you leave books down for your child to examine by himself, or

"Guidelines for Heading Learners in the Right Direction"

if you buy books for him alone as gifts, rewards, surprises, or shopping present, he will know that reading is valuable.

Building a proper reading foundation takes years. You cannot rush to it when Johnny starts school and expect immediate results. Talking to and reading to the very young child on a daily basis will gradually build the skills listed under essentials, and the incidentals to successful reading must also begin with the very young child long before he starts school... In committing yourself to building this foundation, you will learn to take the time to explain words or sounds that are not clear to your child. You will also develop techniques of teaching him that work and show results.

A proper reading foundation is necessary for able-bodied readers.

Reasoning Situations

Encourage your child of any age to develop his reasoning abilities. Reasoning entails making sense out of a situation and bringing logic to bear on a set of facts.

Following are examples of how-to set up question or problems that require reasoning:

- Give Molly a set of facts and allow her to draw a conclusion: All seeds contain baby plants. Plants have many ways of sending their seeds to far away places. Wind carries some seeds; people carry seeds; water carries some seeds; animals carry seeds. A tiny island is far from land, but it has trees growing on it. How do you suppose the trees got there?

- Give Tommy instructions:

PARENTING for Education

1. Use short sticks to build your house. (You have given him a pile of long sticks.)

2. Hand crumbs to the birds, Tommy. (Two whole slices of bread are on the table.)

- Set up physical obstacle courses. Arrange a starting point and a finishing point.

- Present him with physically unequal circumstances. His task is to make them equal.

Circumstance 1: Two water pails – 1 empty, 1 half full.

Circumstance 2: Two slices of bread – 1 buttered, 1 unbuttered.

- Acquaint Richard with riddles.

- Provide Jarissa with games. All sorts of board games are on the market for preschool children. Candy land Bingo, checkers, Toss Across, Trouble, etc. Building toys and games are especially good. Any game can be instrumental in teaching the young child to reason. To get the most from it, an adult or older child should play these games with the child.

Simple games like "Which hand is it hiding in" or "Guess this" or "Find-it" serve purposes in reasoning. Treasure hunts are wonderful when kept simple enough for the child's age group.

- Assign Eleuterio with an everyday task. Even two and three year olds can have chores as long as the parent keeps an open mind. Picking up after himself,

Returning toys to their assigned places, wiping up spilled milk, and picking up paper from floor before parent vacuums are possibilities.

"Guidelines for Heading Learners in the Right Direction"

A regular chore or an expected chore that results from his actions teaches him small, incidental reasoning skills.

Opportunities to engage your child's reasoning skills surround you. Look and you will be surprised. Have fun and extend patience as you practice some of the above reasoning activities.

Training Memory

To spur the memory and get it kicking, there must be interest and usefulness. The young child and the school age child benefit from memory training.

The first step in training the memory is isolation.

Is it a name or a face you want the child to remember? Is it a fact, a numerical formula, a scientific equation, a historical event that needs to be committed to memory? Teach him to isolate. For example: Hand the child a picture containing five or more faces. Let him look at the entire picture for a few seconds. Now point out one face in the picture. Ask him to look carefully at the face for a minute. Take the picture away.

Ask him for some details about that face: Face shape? Can he name any unusual feature? What was the color of hair? Did he notice the color of eyes? How much hair? Was there anything distinctive about the person's teeth? How well did he do?

Now, hand the picture back to him. Ask him to mark X on the face for memory. Ask him all the questions you asked before.

Encourage your child to tell you a story about the face he sees. The next day see if he has memorized that face

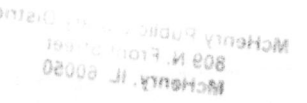

PARENTING for Education

The process he went through is called isolation. He has eliminated all other faces from importance and concentrated on that single face.

This is the first step to take in teaching your child to memorize anything. Won't you try face memorizing with your child?

Vocuabulary Enrichment

Do your best to enrich baby's vocabulary. Give him talk. Give him words. Give him sentences. Give him stories. Vary your talk to give him a varied view of his interesting world. Deliberately sit with him for minutes at a time clearly "locking words into his mind."

Point out a chair to baby and call it a chair, over and over again. Encourage baby to say, "Chair." Work on getting him to say "Chair" for a couple of weeks. Point out milk to baby and call it "Milk," over and over again. Encourage baby to say "Milk," and applaud his effort. Point out anything in baby's environment which might interest him.

Name objects as you pass by them inside of your home. Name objects as you walk along inside of a grocery store, bank, theatre, Burger King, and all the other places you frequent. Name objects as you drive down the highway. Be persistent.

Call out other people's names when you greet them in front of baby. Call out people's professional names if they're dressed in their professional uniforms – police, fire persons, baker, doctor, nurse, hairdresser, and all the others you meet.

Familiarize baby's vocabulary with names of common animals Perhaps you live in a neighborhood with a fair population of dogs or cats, enough to acquaint baby with their general look. Those living in smaller cities and towns might have daily

"Guidelines for Heading Learners in the Right Direction"

contact with squirrels, birds, rabbits, ducks, and horses in addition to cats and dogs.

Acquaint baby with the names of places he frequents. Store, doctor's office, church, beach, laundry, shoe shop, shopping mall, parks, and maybe restaurants are places he will easily learn to say because he can identify them. Even acquaint him with certain words associated with specific places. For instance, on his visits to the doctor's office, he has contact with a nurse and he hears about medicine.

Enriching baby's vocabulary can be very exciting. You proceed on a trial and error basis, as you can't be certain what sounds will roll off more easily than others from his tongue. Exposure to different phonetic sounds is an absolute must to the child's intelligence.

Writing Preparation

Eventually most children will write. It doesn't really matter how early a child writes, as long as he is not forced or pressured.

Experience shows that whether you do anything or not, under normal circumstances, the child will train himself to write. His techniques may not produce letters legible enough to be school-approved, but he will probably understand them. The reason he eventually writes, help or not, is because of fine motor skills he picks up day by day. Following are some activities you can provide, easing the gateway to writing:

- Form letters with toothpicks or yarn.
- Hammer and nail with children-sized soft toy hammers,
- Roll play dough or real dough with a rolling pin

PARENTING for Education

- Thread a needle and sew, using rubbery needles found in toy stores or craft stores

- Finger-grip exercise, as in picking up jelly beans using thumb and index finger and placing them in a cup

- Finger paint

- Spin jacks

- Handle rice or beans for art & design

- Clay play

- Water play

- Ball play

Supply your child with plenty of paper and pencils or crayons. If you can, supply a chalkboard and chalk. Assemble tops from jars and show her how to trace around the tops. Intersect the tracing to form new pictures. Encourage the child to color in the pictures he makes. Tracing around cups or small boxes or jars prove equally fun. Tracing and coloring in the contours develop the child's muscular control; and he is using many of the same strokes later used in writing.

After several weeks of tracing, encourage her to form letters freely. But sit with her frequently in the beginning to ensure that she is using the simplest motions.

Another preliminary step to writing involves touching and tracing sandpaper letters. Guide the index finger of the child's right hand* over the sandpaper in the motion of actual writing. Repeat this step with eyes closed.

Writing doesn't have to be a struggle for Mary or Johnny. It can be a pleasure for the little ones who have engaged in

"Guidelines for Heading Learners in the Right Direction"

finger strengthening activities as described above. Parents can make the difference.

*Watch the child's natural motions to determine whether he/she is left or right-handed. Knowing this helps you to help your child.

Activities Helpful In Laying A Reading Foundation

The following are activities that will benefit your pre-reader. A pre-reader is any child who is not reading or who is just beginning to read. He can be four years old or he can be seven or eight years old.

I. Eye Training. Teach child to distinguish shapes, colors, figures, chairs, and ears. Encourage him to find small details that will identify one object from a similar object.

II. Eye Training Movements. Bouncing a tennis ball continuously trains the eyes to move rapidly and in many directions. Rolling any size ball from side to side or back and forth trains and controls eye muscles.

III. Watching for Familiar Signs. While riding or walking, you can ask your child to help you out by looking for a specific sign. If you're going to a Burger King or McDonald's get your youngster to point out the sign when you arrive. STOP signs and other traffic signs are good signs to start.

IV. Pointing to Specific Alphabets in Words. Right, smack-dab in the middle of reading her favorite book, stop and say, "Keesha, point to the "t" in cat, or find all the a's on this page.

V. Let the Newspaper be Happy Hunting Ground. Give Keesha a red marker and ask her to circle as many "c's" as she can find. Or, given large blocked letters on a word card, gently tell her to point out any alphabets she knows and name them.

VI. Left to Right Eye Movements. Instruct child to hold up his right hand eight inches from his face (about midway between his eyes). Move right hand to far right. Drop hand. Bring up right hand again, repeat movement. Repeat five times.

Touch child's finger to printed page. Guide his finger over words, sentences, and paragraphs, moving from left to right. You need not read as you guide.

Have fun and he will have fun, too.

Scope Of Reading

Surround a child with books and he will surely read. Reading can provide many hours of pleasure in a variety of forms. Fantasy stories are especially popular among the younger children. Jokes and riddles always interest primary grade youngsters. Informational books, particularly science, appeal to preschoolers as well as preteens – but at a different level of understanding. Sports and hobby books, poetry books, biographies, religious books, and adventure stories have always found a place.

Books that are purely informative such as dictionaries, Ranger Rick's Nature Magazine, or Children's Digest contain nonfiction articles, stories, puzzles, and information that will interest your youngster.

"Guidelines for Heading Learners in the Right Direction"

Whatever the book, we, the parents, are guides for our children's reading, until they're around sixth grade. Through the proper selection of books, we have opportunities to broaden our children's interests, expand their vocabularies, further their interests in particular areas, discover interests, and instill values. Too important to overlook is the fact that books provide solid information. They impart knowledge.

You may not be a book lover, however, nevertheless, you can help establish a child's healthy, positive attitudes towards books. What he needs is your gentle persuasion that books are really nice little friends.

Counting

Number concepts have their beginnings in the counting ritual. Almost before a baby can talk, someone is asking, "How old are you?" Others are saying, "How many teeth do you have?" Or, "How many fingers can you hold up?" Baby is inundated with so many remarks about "How many?" that counting can be approached very naturally.

Exposure to mathematics in general involves looking at numbers and their functions in terms of things baby can see, feel, and touch. It involves adapting baby to an awareness of arithmetic forms already present in the home. So, counting is a good place to begin.

Count his toes. Count his fingers. Clearly call out each number, touch a different toe or finger as you go along demonstrating for him how numbers name the amount of things you have. Sit with him on the floor and count blocks into separate groups. Encourage him to count aloud with you.

When you exercise, count loudly enough for baby to hear you. When you're putting on his shoes, count the shoes before you put them on. When you're taking potatoes out of a bag for cooking or preparing tomatoes for a salad, count them.

In other words, become an oral counter when/where the situation permits. Never let an opportunity pass by you. The more baby sees you counting and understands how you are counting – by associating numbers with a specified amount – the better he will grasp the meaning.

Caution: Start off with very small amounts. Slow is better than fast. Patience and gentleness work wonders.

Do rote counting with your three to seven year old child. Teach him at a leisurely pace to count from 1 to 14 or as high as he can, retaining it all. Get the sequence correct. Rote counting is good memory work and familiarizes the child with the names of the numerals, enabling him to greet old friends as he encounters written work.

Give Meaning to Homework

Students turn in math papers with only the answers given. "This is my homework," Ian says. "I do all my work in the calculator." Although Ian's teacher continues to guide him toward showing the numbers and processes he's inputting into the calculator, his homework display does not change.

In class, his grades are low. "Show your work," teacher says. "My model of how to solve is the way your work should look, give or take."

Some students simply copy the answers from the back of the book. For language projects and social studies projects, teachers often see students rushing to the library at the last hour trying to slop together a paper or pictures they've copied

"Guidelines for Heading Learners in the Right Direction"

from the internet. These projects may have been assigned six weeks previously.

Misfortunate students think they've beaten the system or they laud praises over their deception. Sometimes, they receive good grades because teachers don't always have time to check every item; or a teacher gives them the benefit of the doubt.

"Give meaning to homework," you can say to your son or daughter. "Follow the plan laid out by your teacher. For math, write down numbers, draw diagrams, and study the problem. Make calculations and write down the chain of steps you take to arrive at the number given in your calculator."

Visualizing And Observing

When a child is trained to isolate facts, numbers, names, any piece of knowledge for memorizing, he's also being trained to visualize. Memory is largely an experience that comes from visual images—both what he sees through his eyes and through his mind. If the child is actually looking at something that needs to be memorized, his mind does not wander as much. Later, the mind is able to go back and reproduce what it has seen.

For fun and games with infants and children through twelve years of age or older, do the following: Show the child a ball and allow the ball to roll. Hand the ball to the child, allowing him to hold it for a few minutes.

Next, with ball in your hand, tell the child to close his eyes. Tell him to make a picture of the ball in his mind. Ask him to imagine it rolling and to imagine the way it feels.

A stuffed animal, a salt box, a fruit, anything can be used.

After he understands what visualizing is all about, teach him to observe that same object.

Observing means this—what are the details? What color is the salt box? How heavy is the box? Size of the ball? Were there any designs on the salt box? Was the ball old or new? Was there a knick anywhere? Train your child to look and to study details. With the mind at work, sound and all the sensory perceptions

When objects are isolated for memory, they are visualized and observed.

Reinforcing Good Behavior

Undisciplined children do poorly in school. Their disruptive behaviors make it difficult for them—and sometimes, others—to learn. Teaching discipline and good behavior are parents' responsibility.

Naturally, the younger a child learns good discipline and good behavior, the easier it is to correct negative behavior should it occur later.

Teach a child to discriminate between acceptable and unacceptable behavior through dialogue communication of what-ifs, picture examples, or talk following someone else's actions.

Give your verbal approval to your child's good behavior. Show sincerity in your praises, and he will want to repeat that behavior.

Refrain from giving too much attention to poor behavior and lack of discipline. Sometimes children figure this is the only way to gain your attention. Occasionally, you will want to point out to your child that negative attention arises when

65

"Guidelines for Heading Learners in the Right Direction"

teachers, parents, or others quarrel with or yell at him. Negative attention is worthless. It hurts him.

Look for your child's good actions. Catch him in the act of controlling his temper, doing homework without needing to be reminded, talking less while working, cleaning his room. At times when he faces a difficult moment with peers and walks away from an argument or fight are times for high praise.

Reward his good behaviors verbally or with small tokens.

Show a pleasant, relaxed attitude when your normally undisciplined child disciplines himself, allowing him to feel social acceptance comes with good discipline.

PARENTING for Education

"Guidelines for Heading Learners in the Right Direction"

Make a Note:

What ideas from this chapter can you use?

_____

_____

_____

_____

List the tools and supplies that will help you start.

_____

_____

_____

_____

Is there a time in the day that's good for you and your child to work on this together?

_____

_____

When will you start?

Date to begin_____

PARENTING for Education

Come Back Later

After you begin using ideas from this chapter, come here to this space to make notes on the outcome.

How did things go? Good ❏   Bad ❏   Indifferent ❏

What changes did you make? _____

_____

_____

How did your child respond? _____

_____

_____

What problems did you encounter and how did you handle the problem?

_____

_____

Overall, were you satisfied with the results you achieved?

_____

Did you meet your expectations? _____

_____

69

Chapter 3

Root Problems Of Learning & Their Solutions

"Root Problems Of Learning & Their Solutions"

Antidotes for Failure

During the fall sports season at my school, a boy named Bryce repeatedly asked for homework forgiveness, explaining that his games were away and he could not solve the problems assigned in homework. "You did not have fifteen minutes before the bus loaded?" a fellow classmate asked. "I try to do my homework before the game—usually there's some down time," the classmate continued.

"We leave by four o'clock," Bryce said. "School's out at 2:30. That's barely enough time to do anything but eat and get my things together."

"All the same," another classmate chimed in, "that's a full hour and a half that you had to do some homework, if you chose."

Somebody else asked, "Bryce, how're you going to stay in honors classes, if you can't manage your homework? In honors classes, you're expected to perform on a daily basis. How're you going to compete with me in the classroom? You might win on the field but lose in the academic playground."

Standing in the background, I realized that it was not necessary for me to speak. Bryce's classmates knew the expectations for the class and took the effort to reprogram his thinking. Offering him their ways of meeting homework goals under tight scheduling with games and sporting events, they actually showed him how not to fail. One student told Bryce that if he failed the course, he would have chosen this failure.

What are the antidotes to failure? What can we say to our children as we see them struggle with homework assignments while also staying abreast of sports demands? Is it proper for us to decide that teachers need to become more flexible in their expectations of students during high sports seasons? Should we write a note to the teacher pleading our child's case, asking

"Root Problems Of Learning & Their Solutions"

for an extension of project deadlines due to extracurricular activities?

Antidotes to failure do not wear disguises. They are simple.

1. Move toward a known successful endpoint. That is—if the conditions for success have been spelled out and explained, work toward meeting the set goals.

2. Look carefully at your schedule. Block out time for the required assignments.

3. If you cannot perform your academic requirements and complete extracurricular assignments, then choose between them. Which one is more important to you? Bend all of your energies toward the one that counts in your future.

4. Talk to your classmates who play sports and make A's. Ask them how they do it.

5. Plan your goal. Ask yourself what you need to take with you to away games in order to complete homework assignments or to study for tests. If projects are in the offing, what pace must you keep in order to finish the project on time, in light of your busy schedule?

Fix the Problem. Encourage the Child.

Children know when they're not learning. When they participate in an activity designed to teach them a particular concept or they're shown how something works but nothing trickles into their thinking receptacles, they feel as though a rubber ball hit against a brick wall. Frustration wells up inside of them; sometimes, resentment follows. If we hear them say, "I don't understand" or "I don't get this" or "This is too hard," we need to fix the problem. Fix the problem and encourage the child.

Of course, fixing a learning problem is not always easy. Begin by using simple communication techniques that will allow your child to relax and trust you. Full eye contact, a pat on the back, a double nod, maybe a hand grasp will show your understanding that a problem exists and your willingness to do something about it. From that moment, invite your child to sit beside you and talk. Ask him/her to explain to you what and why something is not clear. Ask him to point to a part that particularly throws him off the learning curve.

Once you allow a conversation to take place, with your child explaining all things that confuse him, you can pick a place to restart the learning process.

For example, if Robert says, "I don't see why this angle should be 35-degrees. The problem only stated that the angle next to it was 55-degrees. You didn't use a protractor to measure it," you will draw a picture that shows the angles and you will ask him to draw the same picture. Drawing a diagram is your restarting place. From there you write in numbers and he writes in numbers.

You restart the learning process by working together. Involve your learner in movement, talk, and questions. You ask questions. He asks questions. Look to see whether you have an object that can be held in the hands and touched. As you hold the object, you can say, "See this angle and see the angle next to it. Together, they look like an "L." When an angle looks like an "L", you have a total of 90-degrees. Ask him what number he can add to 55 in order to get 90. Did he say, "35?"

Now, write down the same ideas that you expressed verbally and tactilely. Bring the ideas to a form that links everything that has been discussed. It is his turn to explain, to show you how to get the degree measurement, which confused him earlier.

At the moment we detect confusion or difficulty in the learning process, we need to stop and examine why the difficulty exists. If we fail to fix the problem with one method, we simply tackle the problem with a different method. Throughout the process, we encourage learners to think, to probe, and to gain comfort with exploring how and why something works. All of this engages us in fixing the problem.

The end result in fixing a learning problem is that children stay encouraged learning. They accept that it is okay to not understand something the first time around.

Focus Attention: Eliminate Distractions

Does your child have a short attention span? Are you looking for ways to lengthen his attention span?

If you notice your preschooler or school age child being easily distracted from the task at hand, an immediate solution is to assess the types of things or activities that distract her. Remove these distractions from the environment where a task is taking place.

Rolling a ball back and forth between your child and yourself for increasing time lengths will train the child to focus her attention.

Make a child pay attention by establishing eye contact with her and using the words, "Look at me," Proceed to give the child your individual attention.

PARENTING for Education

Set up study places away from the distractions. Radios, stereos, television, others in conversation, and sibling squabbles are just a few distractions.

Set up a definite time period for study – reading, math, map search - and follow it with a period of relaxation. For the child with a short attention span, study time should be broken up into 15 or 20 minute periods, followed by a 10 minute relaxation period. This should continue until your child learns to concentrate for longer time periods.

To get a child motivated use incentives to reward the amount of time she's studied. Eventually your child will focus attention without thinking of a reward.

Much learning is lost because a child does not know how to focus attention and eliminate distractions. Hopefully, your consistent attention to this problem will carry over to your child's school program and gain learning for her in a very positive way.

Task Sequence

Seven year-old Kim blinked rapidly, trying to follow the long list of tasks her mother itemized. "Wash and dry the cups, take out the trash, call the cleaners and see if your jacket is ready, bring up grandmother's ice cream churn from the basement, and don't forget to take the laundry out of the dryer," Kim's Mother said.

Later, Kim's mother felt outraged that her daughter had not completed half the jobs on the list. Are you surprised at Kim's inability to complete all of the tasks?

Kim felt overwhelmed. She drooped tiredly before she even started. Her memory sank from overload.

77

"Root Problems Of Learning & Their Solutions"

The next day Kim's mother tried a new approach. "Kim, she said, "wash and dry the cups. Afterward, take out the trash. Any questions?" When those tasks were completed, Kim's mother clearly explained two more tasks. When these were completed, she gave Kim one more task, making sure Kim understood what was involved.

When assigning tasks to children, do not overwhelm them with too much at one time. If your child is able to read, you can leave a task list in a conspicuous place, advising the child to strike off jobs as they are completed. However, even when making a list, verbally discuss it, giving the child a chance to ask questions or to make comments. We refer to this process as "Task Sequence."

Task sequence gives order to the child's mind and leads to clear thinking. Learning task sequence at home under loving conditions prepares the child to confidently solve math problems—as in division or multi-step word problems—that involve several steps before reaching an answer. Other types of learning in many subjects will also require multiple steps before reaching a conclusion.

Organize The Disorganized Child

Imagine this classroom scene: Teacher Jones stands at the whiteboard explaining how to alphabetize words. All eyes are glued to the board.

Suddenly, the door bursts open and in scrambles Ginger. Her books hang lopsidedly in her arms, halfway falling, and her coat catches loosely under one arm, dragging the floor. In moving to her last row seat, she throws out a few "Hi, Mary's", and stumbles over a few feet. Finally, sitting down, she leans over someone's shoulder to find out where they are in the textbook and what's Mrs. Jones doing at the whiteboard. Everybody shushes her when she loudly rises to sharpen several pencils. And wouldn't you know it—Ginger didn't bring her language notebook to class and forgot the textbook in her locker.

Mrs. Jones felt disgruntled. She asked Ginger to come back after school.

Perhaps Ginger's mom or dad could help Ginger at home. Ginger lacks organization.

The immediate organization solution is to go to school with Ginger and show her how to organize her locker in terms of textbooks needed by class periods. Textbooks should be turned to show title. Notebooks with attached pouches containing pencils, pens, and erasers should be within easy reach. Leave coats and any unnecessary items in the locker. Carry assignment notebooks within general notebook in order to write down assignments. Since it may be difficult for parents to go to school with Ginger, find out whether a guidance counselor or teacher can show Ginger how to organize her locker and her movements around the school.

Mom and Dad must stress a better attitude toward time management and responsibility for arriving to class before the bell rings. Ginger might need illustrations of how to avoid distractions along the way to class. If she's running late, she must learn to control an impulse to stop off for a drink of water or to nibble a candy bar. Very importantly, she should be aware of school laws regarding tardiness.

At the home level, parents can help Ginger by giving her the opportunity to organize family events or chores. Planning a meal or planning how to spend a Saturday would be starters. Give special attention to seeing that tools and supplies are on hand for coming activities.

Once Ginger becomes conscious of organizing herself, many of her problems will disappear. Even her poor grades should disappear.

Unorganized children, like Ginger, lag behind others because they miss a whole lot of classroom instructions and often never finish class work. They lose self-esteem and the good opinion of others in the process, for their distracting behaviors curbs other students' attentiveness causing them to also miss something.

In simple, it wastes individual student time and it wastes teacher time.

Time management

Is that squatter in front of the television set your suffering Jack who's been making Fs in math and Ds in reading? Every night at supper Jack gives you a horribly detailed account of how his teacher, Miss Truth, hates him. Poor Jack!

Take a look at Evangeline. That darling girl is a video addict. Her friend, eager beaver Mark can't wait till he can get out in the streets to roam with his buddies. Evangeline and Mark never do their homework, and they're lost in any class activity. Needless to say, they're going to repeat fourth grade.

At the root of their problem is time management. In school or out, children need illustrations and guidance on how to parcel five minutes for computing arithmetic and ten minutes for locating states on maps. Time is a commodity they must respect, a must for storing knowledge.

For the child who is already a time-waster, parents should begin by monitoring activities and presenting a written account of each hour's movements. For example:

PARENTING for Education

Jack snacked from 3:30-4:00 PM;

Jack watched television from 4:00-6:00 PM;

Jack ate dinner from 6:00-6:30 PM;

Jack talked on the telephone from 6:30-7:15 PM;

Jack watched television from 7:15-10:00 PM;

Jack opened his textbook from 10:00-10:12 PM;

Jack snacked from 10:13-10:45 PM;

Jack took a shower from 10:46-11:00 PM.

Determine time wasting activities and slice off time appropriately to be parceled toward homework or studying.

Scheduling time on paper and posting a schedule in a highly visible spot make the time-waster aware that he is responsible for keeping activities in specific time frames. It helps him to recognize that there is enough time to do necessary academics and still have time to play.

For younger children just beginning school, parents will want to start them off in the habit of parceling time for homework and related studies in addition to parceling time for home chores and time for play.

Be Quick

Does Mary really need to be as quick as greased lightning? She's trying to solve a four-step division problem, and she needs time to think. Mom, consider your demands for Mary to be quick.

"Root Problems Of Learning & Their Solutions"

Dad, you're rushing Johnny to finish his five science questions. To do a good job, Johnny needed to review his notes from the lab experiment and he needed to study information from a couple of graphs. Johnny needs time to think.

Are we as a society guilty of placing too much emphasis on being quick? Yes, we are.

Undoubtedly, there will come a time in Mary's life and Johnny's life where quickness will be necessary. But the younger learner has a greater need to cultivate his thinking processes, unhampered by a demand to be quick. People of any age think clearly when there is no pressure exerted on them; young learners should not have pressure.

When pressure (like, "be quick") is placed, children tend to freeze up, unable to function at all, or they make hasty judgments bearing little resemblance to the knowledge they possess. Some decide, "What's the use? I can't finish in one minute."

Instead of pressuring to "be quick," let us encourage our children to "take time and think clearly."

Later, when they learn to think clearly in processing information, quickness will come naturally in situations where it's needed.

Overcoming Vagueness

Mary Jane always feels hurt when her mother shouts, "You never do anything the right way. What's wrong with you?"

Vagueness might be what's wrong-but not with Mary Jane. The problem lies with her mother's communication process. As parents, we must make sure that we communicate adequately.

When Mary Jane's mother says, "Clean your bedroom," she might receive better results if, instead, she enters Mary Jane's bedroom and points out the specific jobs that need doing. For instance, which of these tasks do you want Mary Jane to finish for the cleaning job? Should she pick up all the paper from the floor and deposit it in the waste basket? Should she pick up all toys and put them in the toy box? Do you want her to make up her bed and hang up her clothes? Maybe provide a checklist as each chore is completed, leading her to a clean bedroom that satisfies your requirement.

This type of specific detail extends to other communication between Mary Jane and Mom. Remember the day Mary Jane asked Mom to help her with division problems for homework? Mom was most agreeable; she sat down ad completed all the problems, occasionally saying, "See! It's easy. Just put your numbers up here above the radicand." Whew! Was she angry with the low test scores Mary Jane continued to receive in division.

Mom's help was vague. It would have been much clearer to Mary Jane had her mother gone through a very simple problem step by step, explaining when she multiplied and subtracted, and allowing Mary Jane to perform each step under her direction. After that, the child could have completed a few more sample problems under Mom's guidance.

Vagueness handicaps the child. It blocks communication between you and her. Often, she's left to interpret information for which she has no prior knowledge or background. It prevents the child from understanding and performing skills that are really quite easy.

Specific detail, patience to explain, willingness to show or illustrate, guidance and direction are a few ways to combat vagueness.

"Root Problems Of Learning & Their Solutions"

Let us examine our interaction with our children. We may discover a very capable child, once we, as parents, overcome our vagueness.

How To Relieve Drudgery When Learning Hard Concepts

What's hard for some may be easy for others. A child's attitude can turn something hard into something easier. Parents can help.

Encourage your child to believe that if a concept has been introduced in his studies, he already possesses the necessary skills and knowledge to understand it. His problem lies in how to approach it. Erase his fears and doubts by admitting that sometimes hard concepts take longer to understand than others.

Along the way to learning a hard concept, explore these means of relieving drudgery:

a. Turn the concept into a game.

b. Construct a roadmap, using information that ultimately leads to the concept.

c. Sing a jingle to remember a hard concept.

d. Bring the concept to a personal level. For example: Mark wants to understand how to compute a salesman's commission. Tell him to imagine that he's a salesman trying to sell baseball bats. If he sells ten, he gets $5 extra added on to his regular salary. Talk about other jobs where people sell. Afterward, put these stories onto paper for actual computation.

PARENTING for Education

e. Manipulate objects that will help explain what's happening in the concept.

f. Learn and understand a small portion at one time.

g. Discuss the concept with someone who is familiar with it.

h. Write down the concept and break it up into small, manageable ideas.

i. See how the concept applies to ideas your child already knows.

j. Think about the meaning of the concept using other words, perhaps simpler words.

k. Look up words or terminology not clearly understood.

l. Allow a peer, who understands it, to explain it.

m. Help your child to understand why he needs to know the concept. Can knowing it affect him directly?

n. If simpler number ideas are involved, review them before tackling the main concept. Often children have forgotten basic ideas and are not in a position to approach anything more difficult.

"Root Problems Of Learning & Their Solutions"

Make a Note:

What ideas from this chapter can you use?

_____

_____

_____

_____

List the tools and supplies that will help you start.

_____

_____

_____

_____

Is there a time in the day that's good for you and your child to work on this together?

_____

_____

When will you start?

Date to begin_____

PARENTING for Education

Come Back Later

After you begin using ideas from this chapter, come here to this space to make notes on the outcome.

How did things go? Good ❏   Bad ❏   Indifferent ❏

What changes did you make? _____

_____

_____

How did your child respond? _____

_____

_____

What problems did you encounter and how did you handle the problem?

_____

_____

Overall, were you satisfied with the results you achieved?

_____

Did you meet your expectations? _____

_____

Chapter 4

Exercises to Raise Academic Performance

"Exercises to Raise Academic Performance"

PARENTING for Education

Tips To Help Parents Select Children's Literature

1. Select literature appropriate for your child's reading level, especially if an adult will not be reading to the child.

2. Choose reading materials with print size agreeable to the child's vision.

3. Make an agreement with your child on books or periodicals that might prove enjoyable to both of you, as you read together.

4. Select some books that lend themselves to discussion between child and parent.

5. Overlap purposes. Books chosen for the deep pleasure they arouse can also satisfy informational or motivational needs.

6. Choose some reading materials that require a child to distinguish between relevant and irrelevant details.

7. Choose poetry or prose that requires children to read aloud.

8. Allow your children plenty of time to choose books when they visit the library. Give them a feeling of the worthwhile existence of the library.

9. Encourage children to design purposes for reading to follow up by selecting books that fulfill these purposes.

10. Choose nonfiction books that promote and develop an ability to gather some information by surveying chapter content.

"Exercises to Raise Academic Performance"

11. Advance children's inquiry skills through a selection of writings that prompt them to go to other sources.

12. Select books with progressive difficulty, as you see your child's reading skills improve. Keep book length in mind as you do this. A short, challenging book may prove more valuable and digestible than a long, difficult book.

26 Ways To Strengthen A Weak Memory In Classroom Learning

What if memory wires were like ropes? Imagine a strong, sturdy rope capable of holding a few tons, and then imagine a frayed, frazzled rope incapable of holding more than a few ounces. To some extent, school children experience this sturdiness or weakness every time they attempt to tie together learning and memory.

Memory is far more than memorizing spelling words or stanzas from Dunbar's poetry. On the other hand, a child needs to remember how to divide fractions or how to mix paints. Sometimes he needs to remember to do homework, and at other times he has to remember where he left his science book necessary for doing homework.

Like anyone older, children find themselves in situations where the memory seems weak. When parents notice a continuous display of weak memory, they should take actions. See if you can help strengthen your child's weak memory by applying one or more of the following ideas.

1. Write "it" down on an index card. Use the card frequently.

2. Recite silently that number, name, word, or list several times before putting it away.

3. Recite "it" orally.

4. Orally discuss "it" with someone else who is also interested in the details of your topic.

5. Study "it" and make associations that stimulate instant recall.

6. Sing "it" and make associations that stimulate instant recall.

7. Remove distractions and allow yourself time to concentrate when you need to memorize or remember something. Give yourself a noise-free environment, if possible, or a soft music setting if you know music helps.

8. Worries and anxieties handicap memory. Rid yourself of worries before you set about a memory task by writing the worries on paper and sticking the worry list into a brown paper bag. Set the bag outside of your work door and accept permission to return to it, after you've concentrated on your needed topic.

9. Consider good nutrition as essential to a good memory. A sluggish over-fed body does not function well, and neither does an under-fed body. Adequate proteins in food promote alertness.

10. A good night's sleep or a catnap in the late afternoon will give the brain the rest and restoration it needs to perform for you.

11. Read and reread an item you want to remember. Reading gives you the connective tissue necessary for recall and link.

"Exercises to Raise Academic Performance"

12. Eliminate medical reasons as a cause for weak memory. Often, poor memory in children or adults arises from medical conditions, which can sometimes be corrected.

13. Develop systems for memorizing names, faces, numbers, poems, long lists, short lists, facts, procedures, or other items by using association techniques.

14. Develop a method which links one item to something very vivid in your imagination, allowing you a quick and easy retrieval.

15. Distinguish between those items that require memorization and those that require familiarity.

16. Know what type of memory you need for an item. Do you need a detailed replica of an item or do need a flashback recall? Do you need a short term or long term memory of an item?

17. Improve concentration.

18. Learn to observe. People observe with the mind and see with the eye. Teach children to observe as they see. Ask them questions as they look at things, requiring them to look for detail in observation. Point out details, which they might overlook.

19. Improve the imagination.

20. Reduce absentmindedness by becoming aware of what you're doing during a given moment. Require yourself to consciously observe where you put something.

21. Form routines or habits for certain actions in order to eliminate some forgetfulness.

22. Have a place for everything and keep everything in its place.

23. Mind sounds. Allow sounds to help you remember things.

24. For numbers, practice the art of grouping or sequencing, particularly if you have a long list. Set a rhythm to these numbers. Let's say you had to remember these numbers: 1, 0, 7, 5, 4. Use this grouping, One hundred seven (107); Fifty-four (54). Memorizing the individual numbers actually gives you more to study.

25. Play games. For an evening of family socializing try this: With all family members seated in a circle, one person starts a story with names and events, and the next person retells the story up to that point and continues by adding another part of the story. The story continues with each family member adding another piece after he/she has retold all the previous pieces.

    Continue this for two rounds. Use this same technique for number practice or learning state capitols or other long lists. Also, engage the family in store bought games of various types, including card games specially designed for young children.

26. Do not confuse situations that require reasoning with situations that require memorizing. For example, you reason in problem solving and will not understand a particular problem by memorizing the steps of a given sample.

"Exercises to Raise Academic Performance"

Holiday Sum Fun

Around Christmas Time children show a greater degree of creativity in making things and doing things. They also show a greater willingness to be helpful. In terms of decorating and baking (for Christmas) this is good news for the "Parenting for Education" bunch, because it means we may combine pleasure with learning activities. In particular, we can have sum fun over the holidays.

Your whole family of two year olds, four year olds, seven year olds, ten year olds, thirteen year olds, and sixteen year olds may enjoy decorating the Christmas tree by sorting like ornaments into groups of threes or fives, before adding the total number of ornaments used. When mistletoe is hung, its height from the floor to its hanging place can be measured; then add the heights of the hung mistletoes. If candles will light your windows, ask your children to see if the total number of windows matches the total number of candles.

While decorating may start a week before your baking, baking offers the same delights to children. When their creative juices start flowing, children don't seem to notice that you ask them to measure out half a cup of sugar or to fill a cup with pecan halves, almonds, peanuts, and walnuts. Of course, you will point out to them that four-fourths equal's one whole cup of nuts. In the course of baking, they may ask you, "How many eggs do we crack for the pound cake?" Whether you bake chocolate chip cookies or snow balls for treats, young children working with older siblings can be invited to figure out how many cookies to lay in one row, if you want four rows for a 2 dozen cookies recipe.

Soon, children make the connection between counting, adding, and multiplication. They also realize that fractions obey the same rules as whole numbers when it comes to adding and multiplying. As they decorate or bake, they apply these number skills at a very practical level and never have time to become intimidated. This is good.

You will think of other number related activities, which will offer, pleasure, creativity, and loads of fun for children in your life around Christmas Time. Do not limit yourself to "sum" fun, for "difference" fun or "product" fun is equally enjoyable.

Science in the summer

For many school children, summer days away from school bring pleasure and excitement during its first hours, and then dissatisfaction and boredom as the summer continues. Parents wonder what to do. Plenty of choices come to mind.

Consider doing fun science. Fun science taps every child's curiosity and may lead to lasting interest. You can perform some science experiments without going into a lot of detailed explanations. In fact, you will hear your children shout, "Wow! That's neat!" Within minutes, they are simultaneously asking you questions and answering their own. They will probably want to go to the library to borrow books, which will shed new light on the topic of the experiment. Actually, observations are very important for this type of experiment. While it can interest a wide range of age groups, it may involve your twelve-year-old daughter in observing plus notetaking, but it will only require your six year-old son to observe at a watch and talk level.

Try this: Obtain a four to six-ounce glass baby bottle that has a one inch neck or mouth, a small saucepan half-filled with water, a balloon that will fit the mouth of the bottle, a hot plate, and a thermometer. Place the glass bottle with its balloon covered neck into the saucepan; and then place

"Exercises to Raise Academic Performance"

the saucepan onto the hot plate. Turn on the hot plate. Observe the temperature changes of the water over the next five minutes. What happens to the balloon? Children under sixteen years of age should never perform this experiment without adult supervision. Caution children about touching hot objects.

When you complete this experiment, tell your children they have just observed what happens to the amount (volume) of a gas as temperature rises. Ask them did they realize that air is a mixture of gases.

If your children like plants or animals, perhaps they would enjoy a science exploration of living things instead of the above experiment. Show them how to start a leaf collection or take them to the zoo to observe the difference between animals that live in cold climates and those that live in warm climates.

Science explorations provide a wonderful fun learning adventure for summer's children. Enjoy yourself!

Reading That You Act Out

Who can resist a game? Throw in a little drama, too, and you've got a first rate drama-game called "Act It Out." You will make ten or more 5" X 7" cards, each bearing a different command.

That's it. Hold up a card and instruct Betsy to do what the card says. Follow this action with a minimum of five cards. Each time she correctly follows the instruction on the card, she receives a gold point.

What's on the card? Each card gives a one-word command. Bite! Run! Stand! Jump! Or, maybe you will use two-word commands, like the following: Hit ball! Tell story! Sing song!

Knock twice! Or, use three-word commands. Lift your leg! Brush my hair! Write a number!

When shown the card, your child has to obey the command and act out words printed on the card (s). After accumulating a certain number or gold points, your child receives a reward.

Visual communication to promote reading can be a lively, joyful activity. Show as much creativity as you wish in designing cards. Size of lettering and color of cards stimulate children's senses. Take care to use short or medium sized words. If words are too long for children to decipher, they miss the thrill of learning in a new way.

Educational Games

Playtime is very important to young minds. It allows creative, intellectual expression as well as motor development. And, we, parents should not intrude on playtime with our suggestions and our ways of doing—most of the time. Playtime without intrusion is called "Free Play."

At other playtimes we can introduce our children to educational games. Educational games educate. They possess built-in strategies for awakening or developing specific skills. Some of these games require parental guidance, others the child is self-directed.

What can educational games teach?

1. Color for the preschooler. For example: You and your child can make a game of finding all the blue towels in the linen closet.

2. Counting and number recognition. Example: Ask your child to find two shoes that look alike. Or challenge your child to stack sets of three (3) books faster than you.

"Exercises to Raise Academic Performance"

> For number recognition, collect pictures that contain an easily determined number of things and write the numeral beneath these things.

> 3. Thinking and reasoning. Example: Bingo, checkers, mazes, puzzles, connect four, and other store-bought games can be taught to children as young as three years old.

> 4. Memory. Example: Card games, flash cards, Hide behind the back and remember what's hidden games, Show me and I'll do it games, and number tile games that call for one player to pick up several tiles while the partner guesses which tiles disappeared.

> 5. Music recognition. Using a CD player or other recording device, play a few lyrics of a familiar song. Turn off the music. Now, ask your child to hum the tune he heard.

When selecting educational games, here are a few considerations:

1. Age group. Select games that are appropriate for your child's age.

2. Level of difficulty. No educational game should be so hard that it discourages or bores the child. Quite often, parents need to work through games to make sure they understand them well enough to demonstrate to a child.

3. Time factor. If it is too long, the child becomes wiggly and will refuse to play the game again.

4. Guidance requirement. Determine whether a game can be played alone. If it can not be used by a lone player, will you be available to assist the child or show your child what to do? Can an older child or another family member play with the child using this game?

5. Accessibility. Can the child easily access the game? If the game can be easily reached or easily handled, chances are that he will want to play with the game again.

6. What about storage? Whose responsibility will it be to maintain neatness of game?

Incorporate educational games into your child's life pleasures.

Classroom Success Strategies

From Day One Keesha made the honor roll. Every day she brings textbook, notebook, pencils, and pens to class. If she needs a calculator, ruler, protractor, notecards, or compass, she packs them in a zippered bag inside her notebook. She completed her homework last night. In case there should be a pop quiz or a planned test, she refreshes her memory by looking over notes during the lag time before the teacher actually starts teaching. When the teacher begins, Keesha listens with rapt attention, attempting to understand the important points before she takes any notes. If information is written on a visual, like the overhead screen, the whiteboard, or television monitor, she copies it. She knows how to ask questions in a respectful tone of voice.

Somewhere along her educational route, Keesha learned to manage her time wisely inside of the classroom. She considers it a waste of her time to chat frivolously, walk around the classroom, or to engage in arguments or other show-off tactics. She avoids sitting near any troublemakers and pays no attention to their undisciplined behavior. She also discourages flirtatious whispers from Scott, who sits beside her.

Her peers like her. Among them, she is considered a leader. They respect her judgment. Since she studies assignments, she quickly volunteers to perform a science laboratory

"Exercises to Raise Academic Performance"

demonstration or to carry out an activity in her math or literature class. Organizing projects comes in handy as she puts these skills to use inside of the classroom and during extra-curricular activities. Other students enjoy assisting her because of her friendly, caring manner.

Keesha's friend, Vince, uses many of the same success strategies, and he is a strong "C" student. Often, Vince asks Keesha for advice on studying for math tests. While he struggles with understanding a few concepts, he frowns when Keesha tells him to "Practice! Practice! Practice! Practice the way you practice for a football game. Would you go into a game not having practiced? Then, don't go into a math test without practice." In many ways, Vince is as successful a student as Keesha, because he does his best, just as she does her best.

They know, and their parents know, that poor performance is not a cultural norm. A student who behaves without good discipline in a school classroom is not acting out a culturally acceptable behavior—regardless of her ethnic group. Students who cannot read and who use "show-off" antics are begging for help.

In Parenting for Education, parents choose to teach their children self-discipline for governing themselves in the classroom and in school hallways. Parents choose to teach their children correct classroom etiquette. Parents encourage winning attitudes; because they want to see their own children model the success strategies of a Keesha or a Vince.

Testing Success

Tests are here to stay. Their value is interwoven into all of life's schemes for progress. Most are designed to measure specific skills within a subject area, and the results are used to map out individual learning programs.

Commonly, when children mention to parents they are having a test, they're referring to teacher-made tests. These tests generally come after a certain amount of information has been taught. They show how well the child is progressing and reveal weak areas of knowledge. A parent looking over a child's test should be concerned about any apparent weaknesses and take steps to see that the child consults his teacher for greater depth or to re-teach that topic. If that isn't possible, the parent should work with the child herself or get help.

Standardized tests occur less frequently. Their purpose is to measure student performance in relation to students elsewhere taking the same test. It is a uniform measure irrespective of teachers, schools, or districts.

In that category, you have achievement tests and aptitude tests. Achievement tests measure how much the child has already learned in a subject, and it compares how much he has learned with respect to other students.

Reading, mathematics, spelling, language, science, and social studies are subject areas generally measured.

Aptitude tests measure a student's ability to learn in school. A wide range of skills considered necessary for success in subject areas are tested.

I.Q. tests are the aptitude tests most of us are familiar with.

"Exercises to Raise Academic Performance"

Although these tests are designed to predict a student's ability to learn in school, past achievement or acquired knowledge and skills definitely affect results.

Underlying elements in most testing are the following: Ability to read critically with comprehension, prior exposure to specific knowledge and concepts, ability to concentrate, and emotional factors having roots in self confidence and relaxation.

Parents have a great opportunity to become better informed about testing by consulting school guidance counselors and teachers. Testing success is important to every child.

Encourage Your Creative Thinker

How would you respond to your child saying, "Mommy, look what I made?" You look. You see that your four- year-old daughter built a castle, but she dumped a box of sugar cubes all over your kitchen counter top during the process. If you did not react favorably, you're not alone. Parents and others are often temperamental with creative thinkers. However, this group of children needs your encouragement if they are to succeed. There are several steps you can take to nurture them and prevent the drop in creativity many of them experience around fourth grade.

Creative thinkers can be recognized at home or in school—they can be curious, self-starters, and tinkerers, able to absorb themselves in individual activities. They put a new twist on old ideas in art, music, literature or science.

Ten-year-old Davey always suggests a different approach. Whether you're playing a game, scrambling eggs or shoveling snow, he wants to try something new. "What would happen if we added this...?" he asks. Nadanda creates new words, while John is a pro at creating games or puzzles.

Unfortunately, their curiosity irritates some people. Their questions test your patience. Orderliness is not always a priority for them. On multiple-choice tests, they spot several right answers, but test-makers desire only one selection.

We do not want their inventiveness to drain away as criticisms sandpaper their suggestions; and we do not want to torch their self-esteem. Creative thinkers need to be appreciated. After all, these children may one day discover cures for medical mysteries.

Consider the following steps

To help your creative thinker

- Encourage them. Listen to their ideas. Seek their opinions and allow them opportunities to demonstrate their know-how.

- Applaud their questioning approach, but teach the importance of right timing and appropriateness.

- Show them how to eliminate the several answers that may be correct on multiple-choice tests and to select the answer that best suits the question.

- Provide access to the activities, which engage their deepest interests.

"Exercises to Raise Academic Performance"

Memory And Learning

Memory and learning are interwoven in an extremely complicated manner. Recalling a multiplication fact involves a combination of mental processes. A child's ability to gather and assimilate multiplication facts supports how effectively he will memorize a fact and later recall it.

Isolating is the first step in training memory.

For young children up to eight years old, isolate a nursery rhyme or short poem. As you show your child a picture depicting JACK BE NIMBLE, read the nursery rhyme in the liveliest voice you can project. Afterward, take it sentence by sentence, having the child repeat each sentence until he says it exactly. Allow him to repeat one sentence several times until it is committed to memory. Then, allow him to add on another sentence until he's able to repeat the entire rhyme without any help. Go over this rhyme every day for a couple of weeks.

Using this same technique you can train your child's memory to recognize alphabets, words, definitions, numbers, addition facts, subtraction facts, etc. Use memory to aid understanding in the learning process.

Memory is very important to total learning. Patience and continuous practice can improve your child's memory if you work with him – lovingly.

Make Long Words Short

Is that word snail or snake? How do you pronounce that, Mom, experience or experiment? Captivate or captivity?

It happens often, doesn't it – children not looking fully at words? In their minds, the word is too long to pronounce, or they think they know it because the first three letters are familiar.

Help is on the way. Chop up long words. Digest only a short portion at a time. Write a long word like experience, by syllables, onto three cards. E-x on card one, p-e-r-i onto card two, and e-n-c-e onto card three. Get child to pronounce each syllable, looking only at the card containing that syllable. After he has pronounced each syllable separately, encourage him to pronounce the entire word without looking at written form.

Now, allow him to bandage the syllables together, and then pronounce the word.

Next, go through the same procedure with a similar looking word.

Discuss the differences between the two words, helping the child decide the importance of looking carefully at the full length of a word.

Try this with many words over a period of several months, until you feel satisfied that the child is doing this on his own while reading or studying spelling words.

Make Arithmetic Touchable

If you've got shoes, you've got a way to teach your first, second, or third grader basic number combinations. It doesn't have to be shoes, for it can be sticks, straws, boiled eggs, apples, pencils, leaves, or anything moveable and touchable.

On a bedroom floor or on any open space, lay out six shoes. Line up the shoes in a straight line. Count each shoe by touching it. Next, your son's turn. He must count each shoe by touching it.

"Exercises to Raise Academic Performance"

Step two: Rearrange the six shoes in two groups of threes. For a few seconds, encourage your son to look, emphasizing that three shoes on one side added to three shoes on the other side are still six shoes. Let him count for himself, touching each shoe as he counts.

Step three: Separate six shoes into three groups of twos. How did he do? Encourage him to add the number of shoes in group one to the number of shoes in group two to the number of shoes in group three.

You restate the addition, 2+2+2=6 by writing it down in big numerals on a sheet of paper. Use red crayon.

Step four: Ask your son to tell you (in words) two different number combinations that add up to six. Next, ask him to rearrange the six shoes to show those combinations. Finally, encourage him to write those combinations on paper.

This same method effectively teaches any set of number combinations.

Won't you try this exercise with your second grader?

How To Make The Recall

In by-gone days mothers clucked over their children's dinner plates, fretting over food that needed to stick to the ribs. Today, clucking ought to be over knowledge sticking to the brain.

Partly, we rely on the memory to make knowledge stick to the brain.

After isolating an identity for memory, visualizing it, and associating it, the goal is to register and retain, ultimately to recall.

The child who is capable of writing needs to be persuaded to write things down. Writing registers an idea clearly in the mind.

Saying things out loud makes powerful images on the mind. The mind seems to take note of self speaking to self.

Encourage Johnny to engage his hearing, touching, smelling, or tasting along with his visual sense.

Rephrasing facts in her own words is a sure way for Mary Louise to remember the contents of her science book chapter.

During the week pause fifteen minutes with your high school son to review something he's just learned. Maybe he will develop the habit of reviewing shortly after an identity has been learned.

Other types of physical involvement – pantomiming or dramatization of a story, for example – firmly imprint important details on the brain.

Let us take memory seriously as we evaluate ways to improve our children's learning.

Create a Mathematical Environment, Part II

Creating a home environment that says, Math is fun and easy," takes conscious awareness, but the good attitude formed makes it all worthwhile. Conscious awareness requires the parent to deliberately make arithmetic forms visible in any household activity.

To make arithmetic forms more visible, set up a math center.

A math center can be a box of material and equipment set aside in a specific location to be used for math activities or it can be a table laid out with materials and equipment. It can be

"Exercises to Raise Academic Performance"

a shelf (or shelves) of materials and equipment. The purpose of the math center is to provide things for you and your child to work with which will clearly explain an operation like addition or any other concept.

What goes in the math center depends on how much you want to create for yourself and how much you want to purchase. Homemade materials are just as effective as store-bought materials. A combination works best. Below is a list of materials and their possible use.

- Bean stick number rods. Popsicle sticks with dry pinto beans glued on to the surface. To be used for addition, subtraction, multiplication, and place value for older children.

- Sandpaper numbers. For number recognition and manipulation of arithmetic operations that are already understood.

- Buttons, beads, cloth glued onto cut-out paper circles. To be used as counters.

- Cardboard, poster board, or construction paper. Draw a number of colorful objects on both sides of poster board. Write the numeral beneath the picture. Hang this in your child's bedroom, kitchen, or anywhere that your child frequents.

- Toothpicks. Use to form numerals.

- Plastic ruler, measuring cup, measuring spoons. Use for measurement.

- Jar of coins. Use to teach money recognition and exchange values.

PARENTING for Education

- Clean, empty food boxes with marked prices. For playing store—number recognition, addition, subtraction, and multiplication.

- Shallow box with cardboard separators. Used to teach division. Fill box with X number of counters.

- Blackboard, chalk, and eraser.

- Colored, perforated cardboard numerals and several skeins of colored yarn. Child will string yarn through holes, teaching him the best direction to follow in writing numerals as well as teaching number recognition.

- Math activity books. For rote practice.

- Toy clocks, Children's Bingo, counting frames, Monopoly, and other math-related toys and games.

- Pencils, paper, crayons.

- Geometric shapes cut from textured fabric.

- Addition, subtraction, multiplication, division, and word problem cards. Print numbers large in red and/or blue. To be used for practice and rote memory.

- Magnetic numbers and symbols. Place on refrigerator for preschooler to manipulate at his will.

- Anything number-related that the child could handle.

It is hoped that such an environment produces security necessary for him to grasp the principles of math as they are taught in the school classroom. Encourage your child to play with his math center, and encourage yourself to use it to better explain a concept.

111

"Exercises to Raise Academic Performance"

Make a Note:

What ideas from this chapter can you use?

_____

_____

_____

_____

List the tools and supplies that will help you start.

_____

_____

_____

_____

Is there a time in the day that's good for you and your child to work on this together?

_____

_____

When will you start?

Date to begin_____

Come Back Later

After you begin using ideas from this chapter, come here to this space to make notes on the outcome.

How did things go? Good ❑   Bad ❑   Indifferent ❑

What changes did you make? _____

_____

_____

How did your child respond? _____

_____

_____

What problems did you encounter and how did you handle the problem?

_____

_____

Overall, were you satisfied with the results you achieved?

_____

Did you meet your expectations? _____

_____

Chapter 5

How To Deal With
Underachievement

"How To Deal With Underachievement"

Clashing With The Underachiever

A visiting science committee at Rutley High sat mesmerized listening to 14-year-old Amy explain genetic variations to her biology class. Competent and self-assured, Amy used models and graphic illustrations to mathematically prove her points. Even her classmates clapped when she finished.

After class, a member of the visiting science committee commented to the biology teacher that Amy was brilliant. "Twenty years from now, I expect her to head a research team, making great discoveries," said the committee member.

The biology teacher frowned. "I wish it were possible," he said, "but I doubt if Amy will finish college – certainly not in science. She might not even get accepted into a good college."

"Why?" the stunned committee member asked.

"Amy is an underachiever," said the biology teacher. She can't make higher than a "C" on a test to save her life. In fact, quite often she makes "D's."

Spencer Martin is similar to Amy. In his algebra class the teacher relies on him to quickly understand concepts and solve problems on the board. He's gifted with an intuitive mathematical sense, but on tests he remains in the "B or below" category. According to his parents, Spencer is an underachiever.

Underachievers clash with the norms in society; they clash with their parents' high hopes, and quite often they clash with their own hopes and dreams. They are labeled "underachievers," because their low grades reflect the work of less capable students; however, IQ and aptitude scores are higher than these grades indicate.

"How To Deal With Underachievement"

Amy and Spencer fall into a category of underachievers who are generally highly creative and intellectually inclined. Students such as they quite often do poorly on tests because test masters expect you to choose one best answer, and these children have insight into several correct answers.

Creativity is a potential that may not always be evident to the observer. It can include divergent thinking patterns, great perception, fluency, flexibility, intuition, and strong interest in intellectual matters. In most instances, these children are a joy. Other people, especially those who think outside the box, quickly recognize and appreciate the independence, imagination, and intellectual capabilities that transcend the parameters/perimeters of the "norm" which are the trademark for students such as Amy and Spencer.

Parents can help this group of underachievers by boosting their morale and encouraging their self-confidence. Additionally, parents should assist their child by seeing to it that they prepare for quizzes, tests, and exams. Carefully review questions with them, showing them how to arrive at conventional answers.

For this child, you have to assure him that his creativity and greater intellect are wonderful, but tests will not measure his creativity with compliment. Here, he must learn to be conventional if he is to be successful.

Incidentally, the underachieving creative intellectual shows up before adolescence. Try to spot him before he loses the sparkle and decides she's a failure.

PARENTING for Education

"Gifted" Underachievers

On Thursday, May 7, Matt stood before his chemistry class and reported the results of an experiment on determining the molal boiling point of a solution. Confident and assured of his understanding of colligative properties, he provided graphs from the computer and pointed out the steepening curve related to additions of salt to the solution. Before closing, he asked for questions and answered with the thoroughness of an old pro.

Fifteen year-old Matt smiled with pleasure as the class clapped for his presentation. An outsider looking in would not have recognized him as an underachiever. Nonetheless, one month earlier, Matt slid on the down slope drive to failure, known well by most underachievers.

Today, moments before class started, Matt walked in and showed the teacher his neatly typed report. She feigned surprise but quickly showed pleasure as she voiced approval for the calculations and text of his report. One month earlier on a Friday, the teacher had kept him after class to issue this ultimatum: "Get your notebook organized this weekend. It's affecting your total output in class. You have no notes for reference. You don't know where anything is. Matt, you're too bright to continue this poor work you do every day. If things don't change, I'm taking some drastic steps."

When he arrived the following Monday, Matt showed off the newly organized notebook. He had made a strong attempt to begin improvement. Having studied his behavior and performance throughout the course, his teacher knew any improvement could become short-lived. What could sustain his upward spiral? With certainty, she knew that Matt took deep pleasure in performing labs, and she used this to bring him

119

"How To Deal With Underachievement"

to fuller intellectual growth, as she encouraged his consistent attention to all requirements for the class.

During the month prior to his presentation, Matt butted heads with the teacher. He resented her watchful eye and her insistence on completing former assignments. Why couldn't she just give him the "F", he wondered. Slowly, he made changes—shifts in his own attitude toward his own abilities.

Matt is not alone as an underachiever in his Chemistry classroom, and he's not alone among any group of young people anywhere. His tendencies toward lower performance than natural ability began in elementary or middle school, and simply magnified during high school.

Parents sigh and sometimes weep over failing grades made by their gifted children. Tests suggested great things lay ahead, but instead the tide only ebbs away, leaving these learners further and further behind. They clash with the norms in society; they clash with their parents' high hopes, and quite often they clash with their own hopes and dreams.

They are labeled "Underachievers," because their grades reflect the work of less capable students. However, IQ and aptitude scores are higher than these grades indicate.

Often, gifted children experience conflicts with others' expectations of them along with a pace or style of existence not suited to their liking. For example, look at Raena.

Raena said she enjoyed being around people and socializing frequently. From an early age, she preferred a late start to the day; she wanted to take her time and linger over a meal or over a puzzle. Reading should not be rushed, if it were to weave its magic upon her imagination. Tinkering with old radios, repairing them to work properly required an hourless clock.

In the classroom, Raena was given one half hour to an hour to take a test, just as everyone else. On a history project, she required one week in addition to the allotted two days. Demands and competitiveness of academic courses taxed her free time, limiting breezy interludes with her fun-loving friends.

"That's why I'm taking lower level classes," said Raena. "Let the geeks labor after class on homework. I don't want to spend my free time studying and chasing high grades for hard classes."

Having managed to wriggle her way out of academic, college-bound courses, Raena said she was able to work steadily in class, make good grades, and never worry about school matters beyond school walls. This felt like happiness to her. Unfortunately, her parents held different hopes and dreams for her. Their expectations clashed with hers.

Is there a method of reconciling Raena's parent's expectations with her own? Is there a schema schools can adopt to allow for the full intellectual development of gifted students who "march to the beat of a different drummer"—students who need a new map that is unique and unstructured? What about laying out plans that do not follow traditional achievement markers as regularly designed by schools?

As parents of gifted children, you will need to explore the offerings in your school system. Seek out information about their programs for gifted children at any age level? Are there hours in the day that will allow for unconventional classes? Are there schools for the gifted in your locality? Find out how they operate before you enroll your child. Your goal is to enhance the gifts your child brings to the world, and you must be careful not to stifle that intellectual potency.

"How To Deal With Underachievement"

"Apathetic" Underachiever

Kenny Peterson had been knocked down so many times he didn't know how to get up. In fact, he had lost he desire to get up. No, he wasn't knocked down in a boxing match or a wrestling match, and he wasn't in a gang fight. Grading systems and other forms of evaluation had knocked Kenny down.

According to IQ tests, Kenny is above average; his reading and math skills were complimented with good grades until he reached ninth grade. About that time, things started going downhill, because of his moving to a new home and family problems. Kenny forgot to turn in his English homework twice; that earned him a "D" the first nine weeks. The second nine weeks, he received "D's" in English, math and science. His tenth grade year added one more notch in the failure belt--he got a "D" in history as well as in English, math, and science.

By this time, Kenny felt ready to throw in the towel. "What's the use of trying?" he asked his counselor. "I get dumber every year. No matter how hard I try, D's tag me."

Luckily, Kenny's dad kept faith in him. The problem Kenny's Dad solved was: How do I encourage him and show him that he can achieve?

Dad's awareness that Kenny's self confidence eroded helped him attack the problem. Kenny felt overwhelmed by circumstances he didn't know how to control.

"Remember the 'A's' you used to get in math?" Dad reminded Kenny. "I always thought you were a natural with numbers."

"Yes! I remember," Kenny replied.

Over and over again, Kenny's dad reminded him of former successes, and over and over again Kenny remembered. Together, Dad and Kenny looked at the reasons for low grades. In many cases, low grades resulted because Kenny hadn't turned in homework or completed a project. His basic skills were still above average.

Once Kenny gained some confidence and renewed his self-esteem, he soon realized that he was not doomed to failure, that he had some control over his grades.

Apathetic Kenny changed into energetic, optimistic Kenny. Look at your underachiever! Does he resemble Kenny?

Where Does Marcia Fit In?

Teacher says, "Good morning, Marcia, dear. My, don't you look pretty. Go on over to the Chip Wips and take out your book."

At home, pretty little Marcia tells her adoring family what nice fun she has in her Chip Wips group. She brags that they don't do much, and they don't have nearly as much work as the Frontier Frugs. Mom smiles; Dad pats Marcia on the back. They're all satisfied.

Perhaps they should be concerned--concerned enough to ask the school, "What does it mean to be a Chip Wips? Is this part of your ability grouping? Show me how you decided Marcia belonged in the Chip Wips. Will she stay there all year, or will she move up to another group?

Find out all you can about the school's educational program; become knowledgeable about any special aspects of the program. If tests are administered to make these determinations on where your child fits in, you should know

"How To Deal With Underachievement"

about them. If predictions are made on her ability to cope with certain learning levels, based on racial or economic backgrounds, irrespective of potential or test results, you should be aware.

Tracking or ability grouping come very early in a child's education. Unfortunately, Marcia's parents never realized this. Marcia was in the Chip Wips, a low ability group, because her reading scores on the Metropolitan Reading Test were low. Bright and intelligent as Marcia is, her potential may go undeveloped in view of her Chip Wips designation. Chances are, she will never move from Chip Wips or low ability grouping.

Undoubtedly, there is a need for low ability grouping and other special aspects of school programs that deal with slow learners. When it is properly justified, it extends a definite advantage to the child who needs it. However, far too many black children are placed here because the system sees them as culturally disadvantaged, whether they are or not. In some geographical areas, students are locked into low ability grouping, being taught very little.

It is up to parents to find out from day one whether Marcia has been tracked; they ought to ask how and why. If it is their judgment that Marcia has more ability than testing revealed, they should work with her more intensely at home, or obtain tutorial help for her outside of school, or ask the school for tutorial assistance within their own program.

Definitely, communicate with Marcia, keeping abreast of work, progress, time spent meaningfully or idly, extreme paper work, what she's learned, and the general state of learning situations. Minimum doses of instruction will only produce minimum learning and minimum knowledge.

In the final analysis of Marcia's two years spent in school, it really won't matter whether the teacher thought Marcia was pretty. It won't even matter whether she had fun or not. What will matter is did Marcia learn and how much. Throughout her school life, she is going to be tested. Those tests may determine her future.

When Kids Need to Figure Out What They Don't Know

Often, parents tell me, "Zack won't ask questions in class. He's in school everyday, and he likes his teacher, but he never asks questions." Not asking questions can pose a serious problem for Zack—not just for grades, but also for long-range understanding. Parents may be able to help their children to figure out what questions to ask.

In my own teaching experience, I've taught high school students, who say, "I just don't even know where to begin to ask questions. It's all over my head." When I hear this, I immediately check for the obvious: Vision or hearing problems. Next, I check for background preparation. That is, has the student acquired the preliminary knowledge or skills necessary for the present lesson? From that point, I perform analyses on a joint language-concept basis. This type of analyses examines their acquaintance and understanding of key terms and other subordinate language usage. Equally important, it examines their acquaintance with foundation concepts necessary for understanding the present concept. In this way, students arrive at their questions in a stepwise fashion. Sometimes, there really is just one little thing that troubled them, causing them to block the rest of the lesson.

To help your child of any age, here are some helpers to try:

"How To Deal With Underachievement"

Mostly, these are behavior modifications for the child to perform. Your part is to discuss these with the child and demonstrate how this can be done.

1. When you are presented with a lesson, give yourself a few minutes to let it soak in deeply. Do not begin an immediate dialogue with another student, allowing you to become an on-looker rather than a participant.

2. Avoid an immediate give-up attitude. Restrain yourself from saying, "I don't understand this. I can't do it." Voicing this out loud disrupts the class and throws learning off track and permits a disgruntled atmosphere to take hold.

3. Take the idea apart in small sections. Sentence by sentence; pour over the words or new terms. Use the textbook content or the glossary to help you figure out unfamiliar terms.

4. In a math or science class, decide whether there is a formula or an equation that will explain something that you are assumed to know already.

5. Review a previous lesson or notes to see whether you forgot something or did not pay close attention to something connected to this new lesson.

6. Are you required to perform a calculation? Do you have the skills to make the calculation?

7. Read carefully.

8. As you review the ideas presented, write down each item that confused you.

9. Turn the items of confusion into questions.

10. Ask your questions.

Teach your child to become a listener when questions are answered for him or her. Listening allows the learner to decipher and pose further questions, if explanations or demonstrations are not sufficient. Asking questions revolves around a process of communication feedback.

At home, we teach our children to prepare for school lessons by doing homework and by reading assignments. Reading prior to a school's lesson develops vocabulary

necessary for understanding concepts; and it also shows students beforehand what skills will be involved. If students recognize ahead of time that they do not have strength in specific skills, they can work toward that strength with the teacher or another knowledgeable source. For our part, as parents, we answer children's needs as best we can, but we may have to point out to them that this is something they need to ask of the teacher.

Nanette Slipped Through The Tracks

Nanette reached her junior year in high school before discovering she could really learn, after all. Throughout her school years poor grades flagged every report card, and teacher expectations diminished with each passing year. At home, her parents resolved to accept her poor performance.

Because her friends attended another school, they knew nothing of "Dizzy Nanette," the name given to her by her classmates. Actually, nothing much had ever interested Nanette. Books, computers, new educational technology and teachers bored her.

"How To Deal With Underachievement"

Accidentally, she was assigned to an honors math program. In this class the teacher assumed Nanette knew theorems and how to apply them. New classmates assumed she fit into their think tank of learners. Too embarrassed to dispel the myth of a Nanette who could learn, Nanette saved face. She actually opened her textbook and worked. Fortunately, first term ended before counselors realized poor Nanette slipped through some tracks/cracks. Expecting to hear horror stories but prepared to apologize and set things right, they sent for Nanette. Nanette appeared, smiling. Good Grades!

We hate to think of our children as passengers on a school train with a destination of failure, but sometimes it happens. We cannot always prevent failure's occurrence, but we can try. Two major tactics to use as we parent for education are the following:

- Set clear, realistic expectations of each child regarding learning performance. Usually, children quickly cultivate success habits, if their major goal is to learn.

- Expose children to varied learning opportunities at an early age, allowing them to accept academic challenges and to meet new ideas. In this way, they become accustomed to thinking and planning in situations where there are no quick, easy answers. They gain confidence in their own abilities.

Close the Educational Gap With Better Classroom Discipline

In this age of lightning quick technology and new innovative programs for all types of schools, the criterion for learning remains pretty basic. Regardless of how bright children are, they have difficulty answering questions on tests if the questions are unfamiliar. In order to learn and apply what they have learned, children need exposure.

Unfortunately, when children disrupt the learning environment by creating noise, arguments, unrelated play, and other behavioral problems, they diminish their exposure to learning. By daily practicing poor classroom discipline, children reduce their learning content to maybe 1/10 of the average, well-behaved youngster.

Over a year's term, consider the loss of learning that occurs for poorly behaved children. Furthermore, consider the loss of learning for all children in a classroom where the teacher has to manage even a handful of disruptive aggravators. Typically, if Max Mouth has earned a reputation as "a discipline problem," it would be suicide to place him in a classroom of achievers. So, eventually, a majority of Max Mouths may end up in the same class. The outcome is that Max and his buddies set up a failure network.

As parents, we want to watch out for Max Mouth. Is my sweet little Breana Kay a discipline problem? Did I pay attention to the note I received about Sugar throwing spitballs? How many times did Junior cough and laugh during the reading assignment? You thought the teacher exaggerated the importance of this juvenile prank. Actually, you thought it was kind of cute. Oh! What was Aya's reason for asking to go to the bathroom fifteen times? It was not that she needed to go, but it made good fuss-box material for classroom disruption.

"How To Deal With Underachievement"

Whether your child is an elementary pupil, a middle school youngster, or a high school student, he is your responsibility. You want your child's behavior to be conducive to his ability to learn in the classroom.

Although poor classroom discipline will not account for all low test performances by students, it is among the reasons easily checked and corrected by parents. It gathers a cumulative effect over the course of grade-to-grade progression. Each year, Max Mouth learns less and less, because he has less foundation to build new information.

Let us ask our children to become accountable for their actions in the classroom. Let us ask them for responsibility in maintaining good discipline.

Close the Achievement Gap: Another Visit With Discipline"

On graduation day, around 13,000 high school seniors across Florida did not receive diplomas. They had failed the Florida Comprehensive Assessment Test (FCAT). In Miami-Dade, half of the black seniors failed the FCAT. Probably, there were many reasons for their failure.

At lower educational rungs, black students suffer higher failure rates than their white counterparts. Advocates for student learning question how to close the widening educational gap. Some question the fairness of tests that deprive African American children of achievement.

If tests can be viewed as the critical endpoint in the achievement system, then the acquisition of knowledge from primarily school and classroom sources can be viewed as the starting point.

PARENTING for Education

When learners enter any classroom, their behavior and discipline determine how much they learn and to what extent. Both quantity and quality of knowledge acquisition can rest upon classroom behavior.

Several weeks before FCAT Testing began in a Florida middle school, one teacher challenged students to see if changing their behaviors would change their FCAT scores. The teacher pointed out results of an experiment she ran with her five classes. Giving all five groups the same lesson, the poorly disciplined group completed only a small percentage of the varied assignment. Her best-disciplined group scored highest.

Observing her gifted group closely, the teacher noted their good listening skills, their cooperative attitudes, and their willingness to engage critical thinking skills. She asked her poorly disciplined group to simulate these three behaviors for a few weeks.

Inside of two weeks, strange things happened. One girl moved away from her best friend and relocated to a socially isolated spot in the classroom. She listened attentively, asked questions, and found she enjoyed thinking about ideas and reading. When she took the FCAT, her scores surpassed the minimum requirement and were higher than her previous results.

Perhaps, a focused and disciplined effort needs to start as early as possible. Kindergarten is not too early.

As we seek to close the educational gap, we, as parents for education, should redouble our efforts to teach our children self-discipline and good behavior in the classroom. Our attention to this learning factor starts early. Senior high may be too late to save children from the fate of graduation without diplomas.

"How To Deal With Underachievement"

Close the Achievement Gap: Ambition Shifts

For your background information, the story offered here occurred during a year when I taught Honor Math courses at a Ninth Grade Center, which was part of a local high school. In fact, this was a note I penned in my journal, so it is told in present tense language.

During the past two days, two African American boys have stopped by my classroom to inquire about taking my courses. The first boy asked, "How can I get in your class? I want to be in an Honors Math Class. I know I'm smart."

The second boy said, "I want to be in an Honors Class. What I'm taking is too easy. I want to be in here." Then, he walked around the classroom—actually, he strutted.

At the moment, this school is buzzing about schedules and course flow charts for next year. Course selection will get underway next week. Finally, many students find themselves forced to discuss their real academic needs, irrespective of friends or teachers. All this buzzing critically envelops low achievers as well as high achievers.

But...I find myself asking, "Why are these boys checking out the Math Honors classes—wanting to stake interest in Algebra II Honors and/or Geometry Honors?" As I probe this interest level, which I have not seen before, I will ignore comments like these: "I hear that you explain things and make it easy to understand." "People don't get sent out of your class; and they don't misbehave." Instead, I will focus on a few other reasons that may have flashed a green light to my classroom.

Reason #1: Six African American students take my Geometry Honors class. All are outstanding academic achievers. The four boys are star athletes, with three having out-going personalities and strong leadership qualities. Could it be that they have glamorized this course to others and elevated it to a "Members only" status? Thus, their sports' team- mates now envision analytical dialogue where you figure out the rule and apply it to good problem solving.

Reason #2: A pleasant classroom atmosphere is something they want. Mrs. O does not yell. She looks at you, and you have to figure which look she is giving you.

Reason #3: An African American teacher teaches this course, and I might have a chance of somebody recognizing my true abilities.

Well! What is the point of "Ambition Shifts?" Perhaps, in our Parenting for Education roles, we can assist shifting ambitions. Visit your schools to see if there are any teachers of color teaching academic courses. Sometimes, the very presence of a teacher of color motivates students to higher levels of achievement, even though that teacher can certainly not teach every child of color. Determine whether your high school child considered taking Honors or AP courses, and ask the guidance department for course criteria. Encourage your child to have varied friendships that include leaders, "smart folk," and school stars. Certain variables influence our children to shift their ambitions.

"How To Deal With Underachievement"

"Unaware Optimist" Underachiever

"Sara only told me about the 95's and 100's she received in math," one mother said, "but she completely ignored the 47 and 64." Indeed! Sara had balled up the test papers with grades below B's. She chose to see what she wanted, deceiving herself and her mother in the process. Perhaps she expected a magic wand to wave away her bad grades.

During elementary school Sara grew used to A's on her report cards. Her success seemed guaranteed for life. Unfortunately, Sara was so much attuned to interpreting signs of success, she could not/would not recognize the danger signs of failure.

The "Unaware Optimist" belongs to a category of underachievers who aren't aware when they're in trouble. Try to catch them before they suffer serious a setback. Usually, their problem stems from not studying thoroughly, not preparing sufficiently for quizzes or tests, not managing their time and efforts efficiently, and overestimating their knowledge.

Parents of the "Unaware Optimist" have experienced much let down, thinking Sara was going to make the honor roll, only to find she's barely hanging on. To steer Sara in the right direction, insist on her recording every grade she makes in every subject. Start her in the habit of reviewing and analyzing previous quizzes or tests from each subject; this shows her the teacher's style of questioning and where and how emphasis is placed. Monitor Sara's performance on a daily basis, forcing her to admit that work toward grades takes place every day she's in class.

Some experts ask, "How much time does Sara spend outside of the classroom? Does she listen in class, afterward feeling she has understood, and decides she doesn't need to study or do anything extra?"

When parents of the "Unaware Optimist" answer those questions, they sometimes tap the spring of Sara's deception.

Prepare Children to Test Successfully

How do you prepare children to test successfully? How do you assist your sons and daughters in revealing their knowledge of math, English, social studies, or science? You've heard your child discuss social studies projects or science labs; and you are certain she understood them. Your son's use of the English language always delights you.

What you want for your children is to have their knowledge strengths show up on tests. Often two invisible problems prevent success: challenges of behavioral performance and skill-building practices.

Although hands-on learning exerts a powerful force on learning retention skills, most standardized tests still require paper-pencil or computer expertise. On these tests, many children confront several new challenges of behavioral performance that deprive them of showing their best. What are these challenges and what can you do about them?

Sustained Sitting. How often are children required to sit in one place for over half an hour engaged in thinking processes? Not often, but you can give your child periodic enjoyable tasks that require sustained sitting. Reading very simple books. Looking through works of art. Coloring. Assembling a craft. Completing pages of simple addition. Playing computer math or other computer academics.

Intense Listening to a Set of Instructions. At this time a testing professional orally presents directions for taking the test, and the child tries hard to listen and to remember what he's supposed to do. You can prepare him with audio dance

"How To Deal With Underachievement"

lessons or with other audio lessons or games, which encourage him to listen and to follow through with some action.

Concentrated Reading and Decision-making. Regardless of prior background, you child is expected to read through pages of material and make decisions. You can occasionally play games, like monopoly or encourage basketball video games, which lead to decision-making. Also, investigate computer stores for younger children, as many of these expect responses throughout the presentation.

Speeded-up Responses. The child might hear an instruction like this: "You have ten minutes to choose the one word which best fits in with the meaning of the sentence as a whole. There are twenty questions." Frequently, time is not a factor in class work he has experienced. Teacher-made tests, occurring weekly or at the end of a marking period, generally allow for reasonable completion time based on information tested. You can use the questions at the end of a textbook chapter to help. Spend fifteen minutes per day encouraging your child to answer questions from a previously studied chapter in science. Start him on the assignment and time him. Do this a couple of weeks before testing starts.

In your Parenting For Education role you explore ways to assist your child in showing his/her best on a test. If you're the parent of a high school junior, you're working on quick fixes, but if you're the parent of a six year-old, you are planning long-term skill building for test taking.

Whether it is a quick fix or long-term skill building for tests, consider the following six simple skill-building practices that will help to raise test scores.

1. Spell with the dictionary. From early years, teach your child how to spell and to locate those words in the

dictionary. A word per day, along with its definition, is bound to increase a child's efficacy with language.

2. Gain comfort with answering written questions. End-of-the-chapter questions in textbooks provide good experience for reasoning logically or for applying fundamental ideas to new situations. These questions also build up the knowledge storehouse.

3. Read daily. Encourage your child to spend time every day reading her choice for at least twenty minutes. If poetry is her favorite reading medium, encourage poetry. If history is his favorite, encourage it. Magazine reading and newspaper reading qualify.

4. Practice choosing. Use written forms and oral forms. Review any manual or book for school-aged children, which contains quizzing matter for academic subjects. Look for questions requiring choice. Multiple choices. Spend a few minutes with your child deciding why one selection is a better choice than another.

5. Practice speed drills. For example, you might ask your child simply to write down a response to 10 subtraction problems in his math textbook. Do this for 10 minutes. Try the same drill during a 5-minute time block.

6. Practice reading graphs and determining information from them.

In considering these skill-builders you help manage some of the natural tensions commonly facing many learners. This management might free children to show the content of their knowledge and thus raise their performance levels on tests.

When you identify challenges of behavioral performance and set up skill-building practices for your child, you move him one step further in testing successfully.

"How To Deal With Underachievement"
Proven Strategies for Test-Taking

How many times have you wondered what you could do to help your child improve test performance? You feel sad and disappointed when he stays in a low scoring rut. Look up! Improvement in testing can occur for anybody. Only a couple of months ago, when my students took their semester exam, many of them experienced higher exam performance.

"Failure is easy," I remind students, "but success requires some work."

That work involves commitment, time management, and daily effort. Whether tests are teacher-made or standardized, approach test taking with an awareness of the expectations and content. Perhaps, you should also be aware of the type of test—multiple choices, essay, short answer, true or false, or a combination of these.

Help your child by sharing these proven strategies for test taking listed below:

1. Don't wait until the last minute to prepare.

2. Study daily in small doses weeks before an important exam.

3. Review notes and/or practice problem solving daily for every subject you're studying.

4. Read textbooks throughout a course to pick up language and other visual reinforcements, like graphs or data tables.

5. Read textbooks for information and deeper understanding of concepts presented during class.

6. Read questions given in textbook and get help with understanding those which seem unclear.

7. For exams, review any tests you've taken during a semester.

8. Make up a test or exam for yourself a week prior to taking the real one. Collect questions and problems from your class notes, quizzes, and tests. Set aside an hour or two to take your test under similar conditions to those under which you will be tested.

9. If you will engage in authentic assessment—that is, you may be required to actually perform an experiment, write a computer program, or apply your knowledge in some demonstrated manner—practice beforehand.

10. Study graphs and charts important to your course.

11. Hook up with a study partner.

12. Ask questions of your teachers

"How To Deal With Underachievement"

Make a Note:

What ideas from this chapter can you use?

_____

_____

_____

_____

List the tools and supplies that will help you start.

_____

_____

_____

_____

Is there a time in the day that's good for you and your child to work on this together?

_____

_____

When will you start?

Date to begin_____

Come Back Later

After you begin using ideas from this chapter, come here to this space to make notes on the outcome.

How did things go? Good ❑   Bad ❑   Indifferent ❑

What changes did you make? _____

_____

_____

How did your child respond? _____

_____

_____

What problems did you encounter and how did you handle the problem?

_____

_____

Overall, were you satisfied with the results you achieved?

_____

Did you meet your expectations? _____

_____

Chapter 6

Special Problems That Interfere With Learning

"Special Problems That Interfere With Learning"

Information Storage And Retrieval

Have you poured water into a bucket lately? Have you poured milk into a measuring cup today? You can measure the volumes of a bucket or a measuring cup, right? But can you measure the volume of a child's learning capacity? Children are not buckets whose volumes are measurable.

It's foolish to say, "Joey can't learn anymore. He's learned all he's capable of learning." Joey is a unique individual. He may learn at a slower pace and in a different style from his classmates. Some days, he may be more attentive and retain more; and on other days, he may have problems – medical, emotional, physical, or family – that prevent him from retaining that which he should have learned.

Unfortunately, children like Joey – especially those from minority and lower economic backgrounds – are labeled in public elementary, middle, and high school classrooms across the country. Much of the labeling has to do with the storage of information/reservoir of information a child brings to a formal educational setting. Many children possess a warehouse of information not useable within the academic framework they enter. What are they to do? How can they function successfully in a system for which they are not prepared?

The solution lies with parents. Parents must become advocates for their children well before their children enter school. During preschool years, the parent must accept the role of teacher nature bequeathed.

Parents, as your child's first (and most important) teacher, you must see to it that he is supplied with information and facts. Share your knowledge with him as he encounters different things or situations. Explain to him in a way that he can understand. Enlist others to share their knowledge with him.

"Special Problems That Interfere With Learning"

When he asks a question try to answer him with real information. Read books to him – the public library is a good starting place. Expose him to different environments; let him explore. Select and teach him information that will lead to a good foundation in reading and arithmetic. Make information available to him that is of interest to the general public and that possibly has basis for subjects he will later learn in school.

You want him to cope in a world where his potential will be recognized. You want him to retrieve and use information he's stored to build up skills he will need to master his new environment.

Are Medical Problems Interfering With Learning Or School Performance

You shake your head in frustration. You've punished Eddie for flying paper airplanes in school while the rest of the class reads a funny story. You've even taken the opposite fence; you've offered him a reward for reading along with the others, but the teacher says Eddie's behavior is getting worse.

All this is hard for you to understand, because your Eddie has always been obedient and attentive. At home, he's still good, little Eddie.

Could be Eddie's undesirable classroom behavior has roots in other problems – problems he doesn't know how to solve.

Medical problems interfere with learning or school performance. Often, parents forget to consider medical reasons. Sometimes, they ignore them and refuse to admit they exist.

A child complaining of headaches, squinting, rubbing his eyes, edging close up on words, may have vision problems.

Inner ear problems may cause imbalance, wherein the child topples over occasionally.

Recurrent sore throat, mouth breathing, recurrent ear infections often indicate tonsil or adenoid problems. Hearing impairment may be present under these conditions and will only be relieved when the problem is treated.

Your bed-wetter may not be as lazy as you think. He may have a bladder or kidney infection or a defect in the anatomical development of the urinary system.

Allergy. If Molly is beset with a fit of sneezing she probably missed out on teacher Jones' instructions. Has the teacher inquired about your daughter's tiredness? You explained that she went to bed at eight o'clock and got a full eleven hours of sleep. Consider a checkup if this continues. Extreme fatigue can be an alert to a more serious problem.

The above are only a sampling of medical disturbances that may be at the root of learning problems and poor school performances.

Some of the more noticeable medical problems demand attention quicker by their more visible symptoms. Of course, there are hidden diseases affecting many children – parent or teacher cannot detect these easily.

Let us be thorough detectives when it comes to investigating our children's learning problems. For sure medical problems do interfere with learning or school performance.

"Special Problems That Interfere With Learning"

Help For Dyslexia

In recent years, help has been found for a disability known as dyslexia. You can recognize dyslexia best if your eight or nine year old continually writes a mirror image of his name and other words, if he writes letters upside down, or if he reverses the sequence of letters as they appear in words. Typical reversal errors might be "was" for saw.

Dyslexia is a reading disability. The dyslexic child has difficulty reading because he is seeing letters differently, thus seeing words differently. He has persistent spelling errors (especially misspelling the same familiar word in different ways). Uncertain preference for right or left-handedness, badly cramped, scrawled or illegible handwriting, confusion about up or down, yesterday and tomorrow are all signs of the dyslexic. But any one symptom, unless it is very severe, does not indicate a disability. Reading disability generally shows up in a cluster of symptoms.

Parents should pick up on the signs mentioned earlier, but you should not diagnose without consulting a professional. The child's teacher, a reading consultant, a learning-disabilities specialist, an ophthalmologist, school psychologist, or pediatrician are a number of professionals who can steer you in the right direction in drawing up a remedial plan for your child's reading.

No remedial plan can be meaningful until a proper evaluation is carried out – an evaluation that includes an estimate of a child's intelligence level, present level of reading skills, quality of oral reading, and identifying characteristics of a learning disability.

If you notice some of these signs, do consult a professional first. At home, you can tutor your child in areas the school program may not deal with intensely. Basic reading foundation skills like sounding out individual alphabets and using word cards such as "an" or "it" in combination with letter cards to form words will help.

Is Your Teen Depressed

Has your teenager suddenly lost interest in things that were once important to him? Does he mope about, talking about sad or unhappy events? Is his outlook one of defeat?

You may have noticed that he broods a lot. He's fearful, critical, or irritable. Janie, your bright bubbly daughter has suddenly turned teary-eyed.

Teenagers do suffer depression. A broken romance, bickering with Mom or Dad, inferiority complexes, bad grades... any number of reasons account for a teenager's depression.

You're concerned for your child's well being when you suspect depression. You know his health is suffering (he's eating too much or too little, he's not sleeping well); and you know his schoolwork is suffering.

What can you do? If he's reached severe depression, get professional help. Spiritual guidance or family counseling services may be necessary if it's not severe but still beyond your handling.

Light depression, in its early stages, something temporary ending in a day or two, might best be treated by offering your moral support – a shoulder to cry on, listening, sympathy, understanding, words of encouragement.

Prod your teenager into fulfilling his responsibilities and doing his job. Encourage him to keep busy, thus avoiding time to feel sorry for himself.

"Special Problems That Interfere With Learning"

Cee-Cee's Puzzling Behavior

On a busy day it is easy to ignore Cee-Cee's banging a slotted metal spoon against her brother's red wagon. You notice her absent-minded, driven repetition, but you say nothing. At six year's old, Cee-Cee can be a handful, and you don't want her screams to accompany her banging should you reprimand her. Doing nothing is easier than doing something on this busy day.

Greg's mother shouted to him to hang his jacket, but he never looked her way. He continued to handle puzzle pieces as he lay on a soft rug only a few feet away. She gasped, asking, "Don't you hear me talking to you?"

Last year, before his eighth birthday, Rodney went with his father to the ophthalmologist for an eye examination. Good vision. No need for eyeglasses. Now, father notices that Rodney still labors over reading. Frequently, the boy spells orally while he looks at a vocabulary card. Strangely, he is able to spell backward. Instead of spelling "is" as "i-s," he says, "s-i."

Children, like Cee-Cee, Greg, and Rodney, pass through classroom doors every morning, feeling twinges of fear. They are not sure whether they will cope with all the demands placed upon them, and they feel rising uncertainty about their own abilities. Understanding subject content dwindles and grades lower. Each child suffers from a disability—Cee-cee, from a behavior disorder; Greg, from a hearing loss; Rodney, from dyslexia.

Some disabilities catch our immediate attention and receive our prompt solutions. Others cause us to hesitate, because their borderline characteristics could mean something else—a possible discipline problem. Learning disabilities are often particularly difficult to pinpoint and assess.

In our parenting capacities, we become aware of our children's total needs. We seek partnerships with teachers and schools in an effort to accept their input about our children's needs, and we also seek partnerships with doctors and other medical professionals to help address concerns we have. Disabilities, whether physical, mental, or learning, can carry serious consequences in a learning environment, especially when these disabilities are not evaluated in a realistic manner.

If you observe puzzling behaviors in your child, ask a family member or friend to observe also over a period of several days. Compare notes.

Follow up with professional consultation, if you both agree that some problem interferes with your child's best performance. On the other hand, although another observer may feel your suspicions lack foundation, seek professional advice should your concerns (and the child's behavior) continue. Through professional examination and consultation, you learn your role in providing help to a disabled child.

"Special Problems That Interfere With Learning"

Make a Note:

What ideas from this chapter can you use?

_____

_____

_____

_____

List the tools and supplies that will help you start.

_____

_____

_____

_____

Is there a time in the day that's good for you and your child to work on this together?

_____

_____

When will you start?

Date to begin_____

PARENTING for Education

Come Back Later

After you begin using ideas from this chapter, come here to this space to make notes on the outcome.

How did things go? Good ❏   Bad ❏   Indifferent ❏

What changes did you make? _____

_____

_____

How did your child respond? _____

_____

_____

What problems did you encounter and how did you handle the problem?

_____

_____

Overall, were you satisfied with the results you achieved?

_____

Did you meet your expectations? _____

_____

Chapter 7

Future
Goal Setting

"Future Goal Setting"

Setting Achievement Goals

In goal setting, parent and child must keep lines of communication open, and the focus should involve deciding where to aim. From the moment your child heads for the kindergarten door, you should be at his heels, leading him to reach for the best within his capabilities. Her sights should be set on accomplishments of basic skills – reading, writing, and arithmetic.

For your kindergartener, you may have to set up his goals and talk to him later. Older children may participate in the goal setting. Begin by drawing up lists of most important, important, next-to-important, and not-so-important goals. Accomplishment of basic skills is understood to be at the root of all academic achievement goals.

Example:

Most Important

Reread class reading assignment after school. Answer all questions or problems at the end of every section of the chapter in the textbook. Ask teacher questions about material that's not understood. Study corrections teacher made on math test.

Important

Stay on schedule to complete end-of-course projects.

Next-to-Important

Team up with classmates to study ahead for tests.

Not-so-Important

Get A's on all my written work.

"Future Goal Setting"

After the goal list has been drawn up, parent and child need to decide whether to work for these goals on short term or long-term basis. Also, decide whether goals should be daily, weekly, monthly, or longer. Often it is easier to regard goals as attainable by taking one step at a time, keeping a short term, short-range view. For example, if your child wishes to get an "A" for the six weeks in Arithmetic, it is perfectly okay to tape a placard on her mirror saying, "Toni will get "A" in math," but Toni has to have a daily goal of making "A's" in math, of doing her math homework, of studying and reviewing. Setting and working for short term goals will show Toni how to achieve longer term, more important goals. On a day-to-day basis, she remembers her goals and is reminded to work toward them.

Goal setting will vary for each individual child. Its purpose is not to pressure or place stress. The intent is not for goal setting to force a slow learner to expect to accomplish the academic feats of the gifted. It is to make the child aware that his going to school has a purpose. That purpose is education. Education takes place daily. Each day she should see results signaling his work toward one goal that is part of a larger goal.

Will you investigate goal setting with your school-age child, whether he/she is a third grader or a high school senior?

A Dollar's Worth of your Time

Little Johnny wants to read. All the other kids in his second grade class seem to be absorbed in their books; they're turning pages and moving their eyes across the pages and going down as if they know what's being said. With each day that he feels out of synch with his classmates, he grows more frustrated. For just a dollar's worth of your time, you could spend twenty minutes with Johnny helping him learn to read.

PARENTING for Education

Read aloud a story to Johnny. Choose a book that you might enjoy reading. Go to the public library in the Children's section and select a book. What was your favorite childhood book?

Increase Johnny's vocabulary by having him pronounce words after you pronounce them. These words may be chosen from the book you selected to read. Write the words on note cards and use bright colors to highlight them.

Listen to Johnny read aloud from the selected book. Praise his ability to read.

Ask Johnny questions about the passages you or he has read. Asking questions will improves his reading comprehension and his skills in interpreting information.

Create reading stations in your home that consist of books, magazines, newspapers, pamphlets, and even a jar of labels. For a few minutes every day, encourage Johnny to read something from each station throughout the day or evening.

Pass a rolled note around the dinner table for Johnny's pleasure. Provide an air of mystery and secrecy to the note and notice how his interest builds up to the point of wanting to know what's in the note.

As a finale to any reading activity in which you engage Johnny, please co-join a writing activity with one of these. Reading that can culminate in writing stretches the intellect to analyze and decipher symbols and thoughts in a synthetic blend of concrete and abstract thinking.

As one who is parenting for education, you want to feel that you have assigned value to your child's reading. You want to show that your child's reading counts much more than a

"Future Goal Setting"

dollar's worth of your time; hopefully, it is worth millions of dollars of your time.

Is College In Your Future?

Who is your favorite sports team? Likely, you answered with the name of a college team. You're linked with college teams in a way that's not always predictable. A study of the annual Florida Classic game in Orlando a week before Thanksgiving, between Florida A & M University and Bethune Cookman College, revealed that more than fifty percent of the attendees were not closely tied to either school, but they had chosen a favorite. When it comes to going to college, it might just come down to "Who is your favorite sports team?" On the other hand, when you're planning your child's future, you will want to consider whether college is in your child's future.

Because of the expense of college, you will not wait until the last moment to decide. You may not be able to put aside funds for college, but you may be able to make a plan detailing how you're going to handle the day when a decision is necessary. You certainly have friends or family whose child decided for himself/herself that he/she wanted to go to college, although her parents could not support the idea.

You also have family or friends who planned from the moment of birth that their child would go to college, and they started a fund for that occasion.

Let's look at a few options ahead of you, if college is in your child's future.

Connect Intellect

Start Parenting for Education during your child's infancy. Shape his intellect. Mold his character. Teach him discipline. Offer your attention, time, care, encouragement, and love from the moment of birth.

Think of it this way: It is much easier to work very hard with your children while they are young than it is to convert problematic teenagers into productive citizens. At six months old, a baby is eager to respond to your voice. Baby is willing for you to read a paragraph from the daily newspaper. Counting baby's toes and playing hide-and-seek bring you closer to shared laughter and joy.

We shape our child's intellect by connecting it to the child's total world. For example, we connect intellect in the nine month old or one year old child by sitting on the floor and rolling a ball back and forth. In that way, we establish a motion for eye travel, which aids development of reading skills. Connect intellect to sports and build memory and decision-making skills. Watch a basketball game among six to nine year-olds, and you will see them figuring out where and to whom the ball should be thrown. Probably, they can easily explain why they decided to pass the ball to Twan instead of to Clay or Teo.

Connect Intellect to Character.

Begin early with the young child in establishing the ground rules for honesty, respect, and other values important to a properly functioning society. You must talk with him frequently. Explain what honesty means and explain your expectations for its fulfillment. Show him that his character matters. Show through actions, as well as words.

"Future Goal Setting"

Connect Intellect to Discipline.

Reward good discipline. The child who is able to restrain a bad temper or a bad mood deserves praise. When a two year old decides to misbehave in the grocery store or during Sunday school services and you remove him, he learns quickly that naughtiness or poor discipline hurts him. For other times children who have learned to discipline themselves to read for twenty minutes or to engage in any rigor without complaint have learned to master the worst inclinations and to pattern positive achievement. Development of discipline leads to immediate benefits of intellectual development.

To connect intellect to molding character or to teaching discipline requires time from parents. Children cannot arrive at first grade or sixth or tenth or twelfth grade without their parents' continuous attention, care, encouragement, and love. Without character and discipline, it is easy for school systems –private or public –to shuttle children to detention halls or "Time Out" spots where development may be delayed.

Financing A College Education

Financing a college education sometimes seems out-of-reach for many families, but anything is possible if you want it. Planning and preparation are necessary. Planning involves gathering information like the following: Financial Aid information from colleges, information on local, state, and government sources of financial aid, information on qualifying for scholarships or loans, and information outlining total expenses at the college of your choice.

Your investigation for information should be well underway by the child's junior year. Know whom to contact, where, and dates.

Average costs at state universities are generally lower than costs at private colleges. According to statistics, three out of four students who attend heavily endowed universities receive financial aid; more than half the students at private colleges obtain financial assistance.

Parents can ask Guidance Counselors about sources of information for financial aid. Internet sources, like Scholarship.com may assist in finding scholarships. Use directories, like The U.S. Scholarship Guide, to find a comprehensive listing of scholarships.

Federal Funds, estimated at $100 billion annually in new federal aid, assists higher education. 20% of the federal budget is in grants. Free Application for Federal Student Aid (FAFSA) is available. States are also providers of financial aid for higher education within its borders.

Some federal financial aid packages include the following: Perkins Loan Program, Stafford Loans, Parent Plus Loans, and Federal Work Study.

With an average award of $2,000.00 to $3,000.00 per year, private scholarships account for over $3 Billion. Different eligibility requirements exist for different scholarships.

At a minimal cost, you can take advantage of a scholarship search service that matches the student with all the scholarships for which he qualifies. Of course, do maintain watchfulness for college scholarship scams.

In assessing available financial sources, don't overlook awards from foundations, religious organizations, fraternities, sororities, community organizations and civic groups. Often scholarships are awarded from organizations in the student's field of interest. Check the public library for directories listing

"Future Goal Setting"

this information. Of course, do a thorough search of the Internet.

Industries and businesses offer grants, loans, co-op programs, and scholarships to deserving students, and many academic scholarships are awarded per year by hundreds of colleges.

PARENTING for Education

"Future Goal Setting"

Make a Note:

What ideas from this chapter can you use?

_____

_____

_____

_____

List the tools and supplies that will help you start.

_____

_____

_____

_____

Is there a time in the day that's good for you and your child to work on this together?

_____

_____

When will you start?

Date to begin_____

PARENTING for Education

Come Back Later

After you begin using ideas from this chapter, come here to this space to make notes on the outcome.

How did things go? Good ❏   Bad ❏   Indifferent ❏

What changes did you make? _____

_____

_____

How did your child respond? _____

_____

_____

What problems did you encounter and how did you handle the problem?

_____

_____

Overall, were you satisfied with the results you achieved?

_____

Did you meet your expectations? _____

_____

Chapter 8

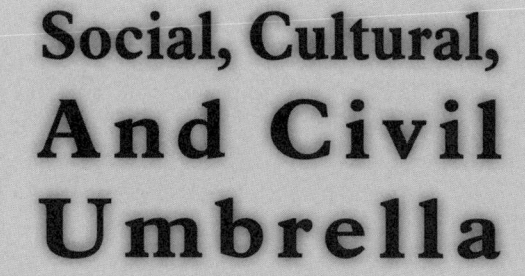

Social, Cultural, And Civil Umbrella

"Social, Cultural, And Civil Umbrella"

Socialization Of Our Young

For the infant who is fed, cuddled, played with, and nurtured by a warm, easily recognized person, socialization stimulates learning. In building a strong bond with that warm person, the infant leans to relate to people. He learns others' reactions to his crying, to his babbling, to his smiles, to his direct stares. When the infant doesn't receive nurturing and doesn't form a strong bond with a warm, easily recognized person, his learning is short-circuited.

Social contacts with peers, older children, and adults during play, conversation, or other exchange set up a jet stream of response from and imitation of human models. As a result of these social contacts, even the two month old baby receives social rewards which act as incentives for him to copy specific behaviors.

What this says to the parent of a baby or toddler is the following: Develop a warm, one-on-one relationship with your baby – talk to your baby, cuddle your baby, laugh with your baby, play with your baby. Allow your baby to mingle with other children in varied age groups, and allow your little one to exchange with adults other than you.

To the parent of the elementary and middle school children, this says: Interact with your child! Read to him! Play games with him! Talk over the day's events with him! Listen to him! Lastly, attend social functions together. Encourage your child to have friends and associates; and see to it that he enjoys a quality relationship with older children and adults.

For parents of adolescents and older teens, there is still a need for children to understand the significance of good quality social contacts. Thus, parents must learn to keep up a warm, loving relationship with their son or daughter. Likewise,

"Social, Cultural, And Civil Umbrella"

parents should also encourage the child to maintain peer friendships, and steer him/her to social exchange with positive adult role models.

Experiences That Count

Tom Sawyer or Huck Finn could set your ears on fire by telling you their experiences. And if you followed Alice through Wonderland, your eyes would light up in amazement, but what about your own child's experiences? An eight or twelve year old also needs experiences that count.

He's in the middle years, far from being a baby and light years from teen-hood. He's at a good stage for learning and profiting from new adventures.

Take him to the museum. Let him browse and search out targets of interest to him. Is there a zoo within 150 miles of your home? Consider a boy's excitement as he compares the jungle strength of a puma with that of a tiger. There's nothing like seeing animals in the flesh. How about a circus or fair?

Ever thought of giving him a bus ride, train ride, or maybe a helicopter ride? The shorter the distance, the less you pay, but the experience will be the same.

Do you know anyone who goes fishing? See if your daughter can tag along. She might enjoy digging for bait and hooking it on to a fishing pole, then watching the ingenious fish nibble the bait and swim away.

A magician's show, a ventriloquist performance, a juggler's act, an art show, a gem and mineral show, a band concert, a play, a walk through the woods, a hike up a mountain, or a tour through a cave.

Some experiences allow your child to be a participant; others allow him to be a spectator. All experiences can add new meaning to his/her life.

Unreadiness In Children

Bob and Jane Foley are typical of most parents: They want the best for their children. They made the mistake, however, of thinking that what was best for their neighbor's six-year-old daughter was the same best for their six-year-old daughter.

Their neighbor's daughter was full of personality; she had good motor development (hopping, skipping, catching a ball, tying her shoelaces, cutting with scissors, or using a pencil). She had a good sense of direction and good eye-hand coordination. Her visual memory was fantastic – if you placed a saltbox, a flower, a dollar bill, and a key chain on a table, then removed one, she knew immediately which one. When told a story, she could repeat it; and she could verbalize what she saw in a picture.

On the other hand, the Foley's daughter was shy and withdrawn. Sleeping and eating problems developed about the third week of first grade. When her mother picked her up from school, the child was crying. Although she loved being around other children and liked her teacher, she couldn't keep up with the class. She had not developed in critical areas of learning for first grade work.

Does it surprise you to learn that the kindergarten teacher recommended to Bob and Jane that their daughter would benefit by staying in kindergarten another year? The teacher wanted her to gain greater maturity before going on to a more demanding curriculum.

"Social, Cultural, And Civil Umbrella"

After analyzing their daughter's stress signals with school personnel, Bob and Jane realized that what was best for their neighbor's child was not best for their daughter.

Each child is an individual. Each matures at a different rate; many factors affect that maturity. Age does not confer readiness.

If you notice stress signals in your child – sleeping or eating problems; change from a normal good nature; undue anger; excessive fights with classmates, friends, siblings; avoiding social contacts; extreme crying or moodiness – beware that the child may be saying, "I'm not ready. I can't cope yet. Give me another year."

Reinforce Good Behavior

Undisciplined children do poorly in school. Their disruptive behaviors make it difficult for them—and sometimes, others—to learn. But teaching discipline and good behavior are parents' responsibility.

Naturally, the younger a child learns good discipline and good behavior, the easier it is to correct negative behavior should it occur later.

Teach a child to discriminate between acceptable and unacceptable behavior through dialogue communication of what-ifs, picture examples, or talk following his actions or someone else's actions.

Express your verbal approval of your child's good behavior. Show sincerity in your praises, and he will want to repeat that behavior.

Don't give too much attention to poor behavior or a lack of discipline. Sometimes children figure this is the only way to get your attention. Occasionally, you will want to point out to him that when you or his teachers fuss at him, he's receiving negative attention, and negative attention is worthless. It hurts him.

Look for your child's good actions. Catch him in the act of controlling his temper, doing homework without needing to be reminded, talking less while working, straightening up his room.

Reward his good behaviors verbally or with small tokens.

Show a pleasant, relaxed attitude when your normally undisciplined child disciplines himself. Allowing him to feel social acceptance comes with good discipline.

"Social, Cultural, And Civil Umbrella"

Make a Note:

What ideas from this chapter can you use?

_____

_____

_____

_____

List the tools and supplies that will help you start.

_____

_____

_____

_____

Is there a time in the day that's good for you and your child to work on this together?

_____

_____

When will you start?

Date to begin_____

Come Back Later

After you begin using ideas from this chapter, come here to this space to make notes on the outcome.

How did things go? Good ❑   Bad ❑   Indifferent ❑

What changes did you make? _____

_____

_____

How did your child respond? _____

_____

_____

What problems did you encounter and how did you handle the problem?

_____

_____

Overall, were you satisfied with the results you achieved?

_____

Did you meet your expectations? _____

_____

Chapter 9

Physically Arrange Your Home For Learning

"Physically Arrange Your Home for Learning"

Use The Kitchen In Your Home

The kitchen area of your home can be the place where your child studies in the afternoon or evening. He can do his homework, sitting at the table, while you prepare dinner.

What to watch for:

Lighting. Any room used for reading or studying should have good lighting that falls from above where the child is sitting. Light from behind where the child is sitting will also favor good eyesight.

Use The Living Room In Your Home

The living room area in your home may have comfortable chairs or perhaps a rug on the floor that may provide perfect space for your child to study. Perhaps, carpet covers your living room floor. In fact, if you have several children, they can all find a favorite spot in the living room.

What to watch for:

Your child needs a quiet place to study. Encourage him to find another study spot, if the television or stereo is playing. If conversations surround him, he may also want to move away to another spot.

"Physically Arrange Your Home for Learning"
Use The Bedroom In Your Home For Studying

Typically, bedrooms are private places where not many people gather around. This makes it a very good place to separate from noise, music, and other types of distractions. Your child may enjoy doing homework in this quiet surrounding. You might want to insure that no television or telephone is used during the homework hour.

What to watch for:

Do you have a reading lamp in the bedroom? Reading lamps protect your eyes for good reading. Keep in mind that lighting affects the health of our eyes.

PARENTING for **Education**

Use Your Office Space To Allow Your Child To Study

Often, parents will work from home and have a business office, tucked away from the rest of the family. Of course, this is necessary. However, consider allowing your son or daughter one to two hours during the afternoon or evening to snuggle down for homework.

What to watch for:

Although natural light may seem sufficient, do provide extra illumination in any room where your child will read.

"Physically Arrange Your Home for Learning"

Set Up A Basement Study Nook Or An Attic Study Nook

The point of making any study area for your child is to have a place that is known to be the "place for studying." In many homes, portions of basements or attics are unused, comfortable places away from active family living. If you can make these areas habitable, your son or daughter might enjoy creating a customized space just for the privacy it offers. On the other hand, if your basement or attic is already being used for family living, it is probably very easy to assign a study nook for the school age crowd.

What to watch for:

You might want to use Task Light for reading in certain areas of your home.

Task lighting is used for specific tasks, like reading. Also, keep in mind that incandescent bulbs provide a soft light that is good for reading.

PARENTING for Education

Use Your Dining Room For Homework

The family dining room sometimes sits prettily by itself, not being used except for special occasions. When I grew up in my large family, our dining room table served as the place of study during the evening hours. Actually, with the usual overhead lighting and comfortable chairs, a dining room makes good sense for children to gather around a large table for the purpose of doing homework.

What to watch for:

Sometimes, you can find chalkboards that cost only a few dollars. Children enjoy writing on these and might be encouraged to explore ideas taught in school during the day. Remember to provide enough pencils and paper for home study, as well as for school.

"Physically Arrange Your Home for Learning"

Throughout the discussions provided in this chapter, the idea of finding a place for your child to study revolved around two basic notions. First, as parents, we want to determine that our children are reading with proper lighting, so that they maintain good eye health. Secondly, we want our children to possess seating that is comfortable. With good lighting and seating, children may find that quiet time studying and doing homework bring a sense of satisfaction at the end of the day. Parents might also want to offer snacks to ease into the homework pattern.

If adjoining spaces in the home are noisy, children will be discouraged from pursuing homework goals. Perhaps, you will find a way to designate specific hours for "Quiet Time" in your home, so that all members can attend to necessary jobs.

Although the cost of computers can put a squeeze on family budgets, please look into opportunities to equip your home with a computer for your children's use. Being able to properly handle technology benefits every child and every household. Most libraries provide computer stations for public use, and many children and parents actually go to the library to complete homework. Determine if that will work for your family.

Many of you reading this book live in small apartments or small homes, and you may find the notion of a "study space" a little ludicrous or foolish. Fortunately, you can decide where and to what extent you provide a study space. Take a look around your home and investigate the possibilities of space that will work for your own situation.

You will find a way, because you know that study space is important!

PARENTING for **Education**

"Physically Arrange Your Home for Learning"

Make a Note:

What ideas from this chapter can you use?

_____

_____

_____

_____

List the tools and supplies that will help you start.

_____

_____

_____

_____

Is there a time in the day that's good for you and your child to work on this together?

_____

_____

When will you start?

Date to begin_____

PARENTING for **Education**

Come Back Later

After you begin using ideas from this chapter, come here to this space to make notes on the outcome.

How did things go? Good ❏   Bad ❏   Indifferent ❏

What changes did you make? _____

_____

_____

How did your child respond? _____

_____

_____

What problems did you encounter and how did you handle the problem?

_____

_____

Overall, were you satisfied with the results you achieved?

_____

Did you meet your expectations? _____

_____

Chapter 10

Plan Your Next Step

"Plan Your Next Step"

Plan Ahead

Think seriously about the future of your family. What is your fondest hope for your little ones? In ten years, what will be your home situation? In ten years, what will be your financial situation? In ten years, what will be your relationship with your children? Will your family stay bonded or will there be fractions? Is there anything you can do to navigate your future?

When you're young, it is a little difficult to look ahead toward the future and actually put into place elements of living that will lead you to where you want to be ten years down the road. However, do look around you. People are planning ahead all the time. When you hear the financial experts talk or you read their books, you could be reading possibilities for yourself and family. When you read information about your child's school profile and talk with his teachers or his principals, you're looking at educational plans that include you and your children.

At bottom, planning ahead for your children's future means the following:

What courses need to be in place for the next five years in order for Junior to comfortably graduate from high school? How do we assure that indeed he does know how to read with comprehension and to solve a variety of math problems?

For many of you, planning ahead for your child's future simply says, "See that Junior graduates from high school. If he gets stuck in a rut during high school, keep working with him and make sure he earns a GED (Graduate Educational Diploma)."

I hope that you will navigate with the greatest precision you can muster and lead Junior to more options when he's ready to graduate from high school. At the end of the high school

"Plan Your Next Step"

years, Junior needs special training in order to secure a job and career for the future. He needs to separate himself from the pack of other graduates. Your plan right now has to examine some options for him that are doable.

By the time Junior graduates high school, he will become his own free-willed adult, and he can meet the financial obligations required for his future training. Your job is to encourage and lead him to these decisions.

Look at training opportunities that take one year or less:

Example: Licensed Practical Nurse

Electrician's Helper

Certified Nurse's Assistant

Hair Dresser

Look at training opportunities that take two years:

Example: Pharmaceutical Technician

Automotive Mechanic

Computer Technician

Look at training opportunities that take four years:

Example: Any career that requires a bachelor's degree from college.

Look at training opportunities that take six years:

Example: Any career that requires a Master's degree from college.

Look at training opportunities that take eight years:

Example: Medical Doctor

Plan ahead! Also, note that extra training for jobs and careers occurs in whatever positions a person holds. Certificates are awarded, indicating that you have now mastered a new skill level, which raises your employability and your salary.

Unscramble The College Process

Fall of the year brings with it the high school Senior Year trepidation of where to go to college, if college is in the offing. Many students labor over going off to college or staying at home, going to a local community college. High school guidance counselors set up appointments to sort through the decision-making. At this point, many families begin to try to unscramble the college process.

Surely, it's fun for students to plan college dreams around their favorite college sports teams. Often, that becomes wishful thinking, for that college may not suit individuals' ultimate career goals and life choices. Ideally, a realistic self-examination will tell the student whether he/she is best suited for a small college, large university, religious college, in-state, out-of-state, private college or university, state university, city location or rural location, co-ed or gender specific, and of course, location in terms of weather preferences. Students may want to determine whether they will be happiest at a university bent toward technical fields or one that bends toward liberal arts. Financial considerations must be made.

At a private school where I once taught, the college counselor always advised students to apply to at least six colleges. He told them to choose one that may be out of reach but part of your dream plan, select several sure bets, and then select colleges that would give you a good education and an enjoyable experience though they are not your dream colleges.

"Plan Your Next Step"

At other high schools, students appeared to apply to only two or three. I like the idea of five or six choices.

But wait...Senior Year is a little late to zero in on college admissions. To ensure getting into the college of your choice, encourage your child to think ahead by ninth grade. During that ninth grade or freshman year of high school, take college bound courses and follow a college-bound curriculum throughout the high school years. During this time period, try to obtain high grades. The higher your grades, the better are your chances of securing college admission. College admission officers favor students with higher grades, particularly if high grades are obtained in more challenging courses. Get involved in extracurricular activities, whether in sports, student government, debate, drama, or special school clubs and community clubs or charities. Plan to take Advanced Placement (AP) courses, if your school offers them. By Junior Year, seek out tutoring lessons that teach test preparation for SAT or ACT; also, take the PSAT.

While teaching in public or private schools, I tried to remind students to watch their behaviors in classes. I encouraged them to show the best of themselves, because

one day, they would need to request college recommendations from teachers or others whom they dealt with. When a teacher can cite your strengths, passions, and reveal your impressive character, you will stand out in a competitive admissions process.

Another aspect of the college process, often overlooked by students until the Senior Year, is the essay writing. For this portion, it is advisable to work with an English teacher, having her/him provide tips to improve writing. Again, if a regimen of thoughtfully pursuing essay writing begins around ninth grade, significant improvements should be gained by 12th grade.

To unscramble the college process, students need to consult college admissions officers and the office of financial aid, acquiring information from the colleges of interest during the early days of the Senior Year or toward the end of the Junior Year. Gather information on local scholarships as well as state or national scholarships, and keep in mind that scholarship applications are time sensitive. Parents will want to pay close attention to meeting financial aid deadlines in order to avoid confusion and delays.

To successfully gain college admissions, consider student grades, SAT or ACT scores, teacher recommendations, essay preparation, and extracurricular activities. When you plan several years ahead, you will find that you unscrambled the college process and eliminated many of the anxieties families often face.

Good luck!

College Is Your Choice

At Senior Year, the great debate revolves around whether Mary will go to college or whether she will whirl out into life at full swing. On the table before Mary lie options of military selection, certification courses that take less than one year of preparation, specialized training of all kinds, or doing nothing at all. Mary's guidance counselors and teachers have already pointed out to her that college is her choice. She is not required to go to college.

For various reasons, Mary did not give serious thought to her future until this year. Her family had always said they could not afford college. That had been a given—cannot afford

"Plan Your Next Step"

college. She had not given consideration to her own skills and desires. As classmates buzzed talk about military prospects, Mary realized she had not taken the ROTC classes offered by her school. The colonel in charge of ROTC assured her, however, that she could enter the military without high school military preparation. When she investigated the local nursing programs that granted certifications for home health care, or when she investigated beautician or electrician programs, she realized that she just did not have that sincere interest which could move her forward. So...she asked herself, what was she good at doing? What courses throughout her school life had been most satisfying?

Strangely, at the conclusion of looking back over her high school courses and considering subjects that really grabbed her interest, Mary saw that math and science interested her most. In fact, she had taken several Advanced Placement courses, and she had always matriculated through honors courses. With honest foresight, Mary admitted to herself that she would love to become a design engineer for General Motors. Fields of medical research intrigued her, also.

Mary sighed. Something was wrong. All the time she ignored college as an option, her school curriculum had moved her forward in a college preparatory program. Truth be told, these were courses she chose herself, because she liked them and her interest lay there.

Sitting at the dinner table one night in early October of the Senior Year, Mary sprang the news on her family that she was more interested in careers that required college than she was in other careers. To her surprise, her parents smiled.

"We knew that all along, Mary," her father said. "We never said you couldn't go to college. What we said was that we could not afford college."

PARENTING for Education

"Isn't that the same thing?" Mary asked.

"It is not the same thing," her mother explained. "College is your choice. You can work and put yourself through college, if you really want a certain career. There are many ways for you to afford college yourself."

Mary's father said, "The local community college would be great for your first two years. You can stay here at home and go to college. Keep the job you now have at Winn Dixie and ask them to schedule you around your college classes. It can work, if you want it to work."

"If you're careful with your money, you'll be able to transfer in to a university from your community college," her mother said.

Mary sighed again. She had a lot of work to do. Now, she had to make applications to the local community college and to map out a plan for her future. One day, she knew she would be an engineer or a medical researcher. After all, college was her choice. It simply took her a long time to see it as an option.

Schools You Should Know

Public Schools:

Nine out of ten students in the United States attend a public school. If you counted children in grades kindergarten through twelfth grade, over 50 million attend public schools. Funded through local taxes, state taxes, and federal taxes, public schools must educate all children who live within the borders of their district. Public schools have legal responsibilities for education of children and must follow federal, state, and local laws. An important characteristic of public schools is their accountability to the public.

Charter Schools:

Charter Schools are public schools that are not required to follow many of the regulations imposed on the traditional public school. They are accountable to local school boards and to the state's department of education. Because of their flexibility, advocates hope these schools can bring greater innovation classroom learning. In making your decisions about Charter Schools, examine publicly reported data on who charter Schools serve, school climate, school performance, and non-testable outcomes. Charter Schools are tuition free.

Private Schools:

Independent Schools and parochial schools are also classified as private schools. Private schools are funded through tuition from parents, donations, grants, and other nonpublic sources. In recent years, controversial issues have arisen over voucher plans that pay tuition fees to private schools with public funds.

Besides funding, another major difference between private and public schools is the curriculum design. Private schools govern curriculum design and instruction, while also maintaining flexibility in adjusting content.

Gifted Schools:

Gifted Schools are designed to serve gifted children. With goals of providing opportunities for children to explore more challenging, creative environments, Gifted Schools may exist as independent centers, private schools, or as a school designed

Program within a public school. Generally, instructional design takes place through a team of experts. Gifted children have unique educational needs that can often be met in programs designed to nurture and support their individuality. Look at the differentiated curricula, enhanced by creative tools that encourage children's inventive nature. Opportunities exist for creative environments, creative teaching strategies, and inviting materials.

Quite often, Gifted Schools are closely aligned with Magnet schools.

Talk with your local school principal and Guidance Counselor to determine the criteria for admission into the gifted program. Find out what educational tools and tests they use to evaluate students. There may be a calendar of events in terms of testing and applications.

Magnet Schools:

When you have talented children, you are hopeful that their schools will serve them well. Talents in performing arts, visual arts, theatre, dance, and music all fare well under the umbrella of magnet schools designated for them. Fine arts schools, elementary or secondary fall into this category. Schools for mathematics, engineering, or science offer exciting and fun curricula that challenge focused students. Usually, magnet schools are public schools, funded by local, state, and federal sources.

Alternative Schools:

Who is served by alternative schools? Findings show that 12% of all students in alternative schools exhibit disabilities. Of the 10,900 public alternative schools, some serve at-risk

"Plan Your Next Step"

populations, special populations, and students who generally felt displaced in traditional school settings.

The most widely accepted description of "alternative schools" is this: A public institution that supports elementary or secondary educational needs for students whose needs are not met in regular school settings. Typically smaller enrollments allow these schools to design curricula relevant to student needs. Advocates stress the value of decision-making by students and greater one-on-one interaction between teacher and student as critical elements in students' success in alternative education schools. Students at risk of failure receive placement due to parent inquiry, teacher recommendation, or regular school administrative request. Sometimes, students themselves will seek haven in an alternative school.

Offering a flexible program of study, alternative education schools may utilize a nontraditional curriculum and methods of instruction.

AIM

So often we hear people lament, "Oh, I wish I could have foresee that!"

Foresight would indeed be better than hindsight. Foresight is really not anything magical, and it is certainly not elusive. All it requires is a little analyzing of the problem, preparing for a solution, time management, and aim. Most important is aim.

Aim is the bright shiny apple the marksmen shoot for at a distance. Aim is the Olympic medal champions set their sights on during long years of training. Aim is the business enterprise George Johnson worked to achieve during the years that led him to market Afro Sheen. Aim is the vision parents can direct their children toward for future goals. It will require focusing

PARENTING for Education

their attention further than the next hour or the next day – it may mean focusing attention for years down the road.

When we look far down the road, we gather some plan of action. We ask ourselves, "Now, how can I possibly achieve this goal?"

Directing our children to the good futures will require plans of action from both parent and child. The aim for a good future must come from dedication and willingness. Sacrifice may be in order.

Little by little we have to train our children to delay gratifications for a while, to wait for those things that are really important.

I am reminded of a family whose story appeared in a national newspaper several years ago. The family said they could not afford to send their son, who was a graduating senior, to college – but they bought him a Cadillac for a graduation present.

Clearly, they were looking only a short distance and were giving immediate gratification. They did not look to the long run; they did not use foresight.

Will you get together with your children and sent an aim far down the road that will be beneficial for a hope-filled tomorrow? Include plans and decide on preparations. Then, follow through.

Choosing The Right College

Will you choose a community or junior college, or a four-year college or university? Private or state supported? Religious or nonsectarian? Do you want to be close to home or far away?

"Plan Your Next Step"

Many considerations have to be made in choosing a college. These considerations should be base on the student and his needs. Naturally, costs and affordability are partly the family's concern.

If the student has already decided on the career she wants to train for, she will want to look at colleges offering majors in her field of interest and which ones offer the best preparation. Specialized field such as music, engineering, business, or the arts can be studied in depth at technical four-year colleges. Not to be overlooked are the supportive services found at some colleges.

The small town girl may be more comfortable in a small college setting in a small or medium sized city. She will be interested in the kind of atmosphere for study as well as the social atmosphere. Levels of competition and kind of campus life available affect whether a college is "right."

Is your selected college accredited? Find out before you apply. Visit colleges that interest you, and ask a random sample of students how they like it there. Ask them to name some disadvantages and advantages.

What's the financial picture for you at your chosen college? Will you be able to secure funds to help pay for your child's education? What are the conditions for obtaining funds?

Write for catalogs from a few chosen colleges to study their programs and to get other vital information.

PARENTING for Education

"Plan Your Next Step"

Make a Note:

What ideas from this chapter can you use?

_____

_____

_____

_____

List the tools and supplies that will help you start.

_____

_____

_____

_____

Is there a time in the day that's good for you and your child to work on this together?

_____

_____

When will you start?

Date to begin_____

PARENTING for Education

Come Back Later

After you begin using ideas from this chapter, come here to this space to make notes on the outcome.

How did things go? Good ❑   Bad ❑   Indifferent ❑

What changes did you make? _____

_____

_____

How did your child respond? _____

_____

_____

What problems did you encounter and how did you handle the problem?

_____

_____

Overall, were you satisfied with the results you achieved?

_____

Did you meet your expectations? _____

_____

PARENTING for Education

Glossary of Terms

This glossary contains terms that you may see or hear being used by your child's school or teacher. Many of the terms have not been used directly in this book. Hopefully, all of the terms will become familiar for your reference.

A

ADHD: Attention Deficit Hyperactivity Disorder. A learning disability characterized by impulsivity, over-activity, inattentiveness, or a combination, when these characteristics are out of the normal range for a child's age and development.

Adolescent: A young person. That period of time between puberty and the completion of physical growth. Chronologically, this is between 12 years old and nineteen years of age.

Achievement Tests: Tests used to measure knowledge or proficiency a student acquires through lessons taught.

ACT: American College Test

Advanced Placement Test: A series of voluntary exams based on college-level courses taken in high school. High school students who do well on one or more of these exams have the opportunity to earn credit, advanced placement, or both for college.

Affirmative Action: A policy that seeks to redress past discrimination through active measures to ensure equal opportunity in education and employment.

AMO: Annual Measurable Objectives.

Anti-Social Behavior Disorders: Disruptive acts characterized by hostility and intentional aggression. A personality disorder marked by behavior deviating sharply from the social norm.

Apathetic: Indifferent. Showing or feeling no concern or interest. Unresponsive.

Aptitude Tests: Tests that measure ability of a person to acquire knowledge. Standardized tests that determine a person's ability to learn.

Association: Linking one thought, thing, or idea to another. Bringing familiarity to mind.

At-risk Student: Students so labeled because they are not succeeding in school based on information gathered from test scores, attendance, or discipline problems.

Attitude: One's complex mental state or disposition toward a person or situation. A way of feeling or acting, positively or negatively. A favorable or unfavorable reaction toward someone or something, shown in behavior, feelings, values, or beliefs.

B

Behavioral Objectives: Smaller, observable goals used by teachers and others as an effective means of achieving larger and broader goals.

Behavioral Intervention Program: Providing accommodation in the learning environment for students to learn to manage their own behavior with positive supports or a specialized behavior management system.

Benchmark: Criteria/Statements of major milestones for learning for each of the Sunshine State Standards.

Bilingual Education: An in school program for students whose first language is not English or who have limited English skills.

Block Scheduling: A method of academic scheduling that allows students to take fewer classes each day, as these classes are subdivided into "blocks" of time. For example, the semester block schedule allows students to take four 90-minute classes per day for an entire semester.

Braille: A system of reading and writing for individuals who are visually impaired in which letters and words are formed by patterns of raised dots that are felt by the fingertips.

Brainstorming: A group problem-solving technique that involves the spontaneous contribution of ideas from all members of the group.

Boarding schools: Schools that provide meals and lodging for its students. Residential schools where students actually live.

C

CECAS: Acronym for Comprehensive Exceptional Children Accountability System

Certificate/Credential: The teacher has completed the necessary basic training courses and passed the teacher exam.

Charter Schools: A tax-supported school established by a charter between a school board and an outside group which operates the school without most local and state educational regulations in order to achieve a set of goals.

Closed campus: This refers to a high school that does not allow students to leave campus for lunch or does not allow students to come and go without permission during the school day.

Cooperative Learning: Students of dissimilar abilities work together on an assignment, and each student has a specific responsibility within the group. Students complete assignments together and receive a common grade.

Core Academics: The required subjects in middle and high schools—usually English (literature), history (social studies), math, and science.

Criterion-referenced Test: A test that measures how well a student has learned a specific body of knowledge and knowledge.

Cross-cultural Language and Development (CLAD): A test that teachers must pass to gain credentials that qualify them to teach English to English learners. The BCLAD is the CLAD for bilingual teachers.

D

Differentiated Instruction: This is also referred to as "individualized" or "customized" instruction—different teaching methods for students with learning disabilities. Many schools require teachers to use this form of instruction with all of their regular classes, also.

Distributive Education: vocational studies combined with work experience. For many schools, this is a special program of vocational education at the high school level in which a student is employed part-time, receiving on-the-job training.

Dramatization: The act of dramatizing to make a book, event, or other situation into a play or animated presentation. To make something more noticeable.

Dropout: a student who leaves school or college without graduating. One who quits school.

Dyslexia: A learning disorder causing impairment in reading and spelling. Symptoms for dyslexia also show up in writing. A learning disability marked by difficulty in recognizing or comprehending written words.

E

EDUCATION ACRONYMS—example ESE, CROP

ELL: English Language Learner=Student whose first language is one other than English and who needs language assistance in order to participate fully in the school's regular curriculum.

ESE: Exceptional Student education

Eye-hand coordination or hand-eye coordination: The ability of the visual system to coordinate the information received through the eyes to control movement of the hands. To guide with the eyes the movement of the hands. Activities that involve cutting, stringing, lacing, and similar movements.

F

Flexibility: Capable of adapting to new, different, or changing requirements.

Fluency: When one is able to express oneself easily and without effort. To speak, read, or write smoothly. To smoothly read text aloud.

Fluent English Proficient (FEP): A designation that means a student is no longer considered as part of the school's English learner population. It refers to students who learned English.

Formative Assessment: A method of assessment used by an educator to evaluate students' knowledge and understanding of particular content and then to adjust instructional practices accordingly toward improving students learning capabilities in nay given subject.

FRL: Free and Reduced Priced Lunch. Children qualify, based upon parent or guardian financial status, to receive either free or reduced priced lunch through a federal governmental program.

G

GED: General Educational Development. An equivalent to a high school diploma. A group of five subject area tests are administered to someone who does not have a high school diploma. When these tests are passed, students receive a high school equivalency credential.

GETC: Governor's Education Transformation Commission. The GETC was established in September 2010 to provide oversight and consultation on the use of state Race to the Top Funds.

Grading Scale: For education, the grading scale is a method of assessment and recording showing varying levels of comprehension within a subject area. Sometimes letters are used to distinguish different levels; and at other times, percentages are used.

Graphic symbol: A written symbol that is used to represent speech. Visual features that convey meaning.

H

Home School: To teach school subjects to one's children at home.

Horizontally: Something placed at right angles to a vertical line. Lying parallel to the level ground.

I

Identity: the collective aspect of the set of characteristics that make one thing recognizable and different from all others.

IEP: Individual Educational Program or Individual Educational Plan. A plan usually set through special education or guidance departments, which defines the individualized objectives of a child who has been labeled with a disability. An IEP is also set up for gifted children, because they require a unique plan to address their needs.

Imitative reading: Dramatic play or pretend play when reading aloud. A type of oral reading that engages greater exploration of the meaning of words and language.

Immersion education: A program that teaches children to speak, read, and write in a second language by surrounding them with conversation and instruction in that language.

Inclusion/Mainstreaming: the practice of placing students with disabilities in regular classrooms.

Independent Study: A form of education offered by many high schools or colleges which permits academic work chosen by the student to be undertaken outside of the traditional classroom. The academic work is under an instructor's supervision.

Integrated Curriculum: Refers to the practice of using a single theme to teach a variety of subjects. It also refers to an interdisciplinary curriculum, which combines several school subjects into one project.

IQ: Intelligence Quotient. The ratio of a person's mental age to the chronological age. Measure of a person's intelligence as shown through an intelligence test.

Intensive Reading: Coursework designed by individual schools and instructors to improve students' reading abilities through specific learning aims and tasks. A study technique for organized reading, which will have to be understood and remembered.

International Baccalaureate (IB): A rigorous college preparation course of study that leads to examinations for highly motivated high school students. IB allows students the opportunity to earn college credit from many universities if their exam scores are high enough.

Intuition: The act or faculty of knowing or sensing without the use of rational processes. Cognition that is quick and responsive.

J

Job Shadowing: A program to see how the skills learned in school relate to the workplace.

L

Language Arts: The focus is on reading, speaking, listening, and writing skills.

M

Manipulative: Any of various objectives designed to be moved about or arranged by hand as a means of developing motor skills or understanding abstractions (especially in mathematics).

Magnet School: Public schools with specialized curricula. For example, some school districts have magnet schools focused on music, the fine arts, mathematics, theatre, or engineering. Primarily students spend most of the day studying courses related to the specialized area.

N

No Child Left Behind/NCLB: Signed into law by President bush in 2002, No Child Left behind sets performance guidelines for all schools and also stipulates what must be included in accountability reports to parents.

O

Objectives: Something that you want to attain through your efforts or actions. A goal that you want to accomplish.

Over Achievers: One who performs academically better than expected, often in reference to potential indicated by tests of one's mental ability or aptitude.

P

Pantomiming: Communication by means of gesture or facial expression.

Parent teacher Association: A national organization of parents, teachers, and other interested persons that has chapters in schools.

Phonemic Awareness: The ability to hear and identify individual sounds –or phonemes—in spoken words.

Phonics: An instructional strategy used to teach reading. It helps beginning readers by teaching them letter-sound relationships and having them sound out words.

Physical Education (PE): Program focused on developing physical and motor fitness; fundamental motor skills and patterns; and skills in aquatics, dance, individual and group games, and sports (including intramural and lifetime sports).

PSAT: Preliminary Student Achievement Test. Preliminary SAT. Test given by the College Board. Also known as the National Merit Qualifying Test. A trademark used for a preliminary standardized college entrance examination. An examination given to high school sophomores and juniors.

Pullout Programs: Students receive instruction in small groups outside of the classroom.

R

Remedial Learning: An approach to learning for struggling students using evidence-based methods of instruction, which clarify skills or concepts. Adjusted techniques and strategies are used to acquire information.

Resource Specialists: Certified/qualified professional/teachers who work with special education students by assisting them in regular classes or pulling them out of class for extra help.

Resource Teacher: Most often a teacher who uses small group or individual instruction to assist children with various learning differences.

Reward Systems: Those objects which students work to acquire through allocation of effort, time, energy, or a combination. A defined set of procedures, conditions, or goals for which something is given or received in recompense for worthy behavior.

Rubric: refers to a grading or scoring system. A rubric is a scoring tool that lists the criteria to be met in a piece of work. A rubric also describes levels of quality for each of the criteria.

S

School Climate: The quality and character of school life.

School Improvement Program (SIP): A state-funded program for elementary and secondary schools to improve instruction, services, school environment and organization at school sites according to plans developed by School Site Councils.

School Site Council (SSC): Legally designated group of teachers, parents, administrators, and interested community members who work together to develop and monitor a school's improvement plan.

Scientifically based research: Research that involves the application of rigorous, systemic, and objective procedures to obtain reliable and valid knowledge relevant to educational activities and programs.

Socialization: A continuous process whereby an individual develops personal identity and learns the norms, behaviors, value systems, and social skills appropriate for functioning in society. A process by which an individual learns how to interact with others.

Socioeconomically Disadvantaged: Students whose parents do not have a high school diploma or who participate in the federally funded free/reduced price meal program because of low family income.

Special Education: Special instruction provided for students with educational or physical disabilities, tailored to each student's needs and learning style.

Standardized test: Tests that are administered and scored under uniform conditions. Any empirically developed examination with established reliability and validity as determined by repeated evaluation of the method and results.

STEM: Science, Technology, Engineering, and Mathematics. An innovative plan to get more students interested in studying STEM related fields.

T

Task Sequence: A plan for the order in which tasks are performed.

Team Teaching: When two or more teachers partner up to teach a subject or center several subjects on a common theme. Team Teaching can also mean that a group of several teachers work together to plan, conduct, and evaluate the learning activities for the same group of students.

Title 1: A federal program that provides funds to improve the academic achievement for educationally disadvantaged students who score below the 50th percentile on standardized tests, including the children of migrant workers.

Tracking: The practice of sorting the entire school population by academic ability level for all classes. Placing students in any of several courses according to ability, achievement, or needs.

Traditional Calendar: School starts in September and ends in June for a total of 180 days of instruction.

U

Underachiever: Students whose in-school performance is lower and different from predictable achievement based on IQ tests and aptitude test scores.

V

Vertically: Up and down movement or positioning. Upright. A position situated at right angles to the horizon.

Vagueness: Unclearness. Not easy to follow. Expressed poorly.

W

Whole Language: A teaching method that focuses on reading for meaning in context.

Y

Year-round Education: A modified school calendar that gives students short breaks throughout the year, instead of a traditional three-month summer break.

Z

Zoning: In most jurisdictions, zoning refers to the streets near the school that set boundaries for the population whom the school will serve.

Index

A
Alternative Schools 201
Arithmetic 22, 107, 109

B
Babbling 17
Babies 33, 41
Bonding 41

C
Charter Schools 200
Children's Literature 91
Classroom Success 101
College 160, 162, 195, 197, 203
Common Knowledge 44
Competent Learning 16
Control 18
Counting 62
Creativity 104

D
Depression 149
Distractions 76
Dyslexia 148

E
Educational Games 99
Educational Planning 51, 193
Environment 8, 18, 22
Eye Training 60

F
Failure 73

G
Games 99
GED 193
Gifted Schools 200
Goal Setting 157

H
Holiday 96
Homework 63, 180, 185

I
Informal Settings 180
Information Storage 145
Internet Use 13

L
Learning 8, 25, 32, 41, 84, 106

M

Magnet Schools 201
Manipulative 49
Math 22, 109
Medical Problems 146
Memory 56, 92, 106
Mental Comfort 10
Moral Support 21
Motivation 29

N

Nurturing Climate 10

O

Organization 78

P

Pantomiming 109
Parental Attitudes 8
Parenting for Education Philosophy 48
Physical Comfort 10
Power Bickering 12
Private Schools 200
Public Schools 199

R

Reading 48, 53, 60, 61, 98
Reasoning 54
Respect 12

S

Science 97
Socialization 171
Study Areas 181, 182, 183, 184

T

Task Sequence 77
Tests 103, 135, 138
Time Management 27, 80, 158
Toys 24
Tracking 124

U

Underachievement 117, 119, 122, 134
Unreadiness 173

V

Vagueness 82
Visualizing 64
Vocuabulary 57

W

Working Moms 7
Writing Skills 58